INVOLVED

Parents' Connection To Drug Prevention

INVOLVED

Parents' Connection To Drug Prevention

Todd Raybuck

Marilyn Morris

CHARLES RIVER PUBLISHING COMPANY

Plano, Texas

INVOLVED

Parents' Connection To Drug Prevention

Written by Todd Raybuck and Marilyn Morris
Cover by Charles Joseph

Copyright ©2008 by Todd Raybuck and Marilyn Morris

All rights reserved.
Reproduction in any manner, in whole or in part, in English or any other language, including usage of electronic, mechanical, digital, photocopy, recording, or any system developed in the future without prior written permission from the publisher, except for brief quotations in printed reviews is strictly prohibited.

ISBN: 978-0-9648113-7-9

Library of Congress Control Number: 2008932268

For information address:

Charles River Publishing Company
P.O. Box 940534
Plano, TX 75094-0534

PRINTED IN CHINA

CONTENTS

Introduction		7
1	Reality Check	11
2	The Importance of a Dream	29
3	Why Should You Care About Drug Abuse?	43
4	What Every Parents Needs to Know	57
5	What's Wrong with a Little Experimenting?	69
6	Tobacco: America's #1 Killer	83
7	Alcohol: The Most Acceptable Drug	101
8	Inhalants	125
9	Marijuana	137
10	Prescription Drugs	161
11	Ecstasy	179
12	Cocaine	195
13	Methamphetamine	211
14	Anabolic-Androgenic Steroids	229
15	No Magic Wand	243
Other Drugs of Abuse		255
Types of Drugs		261

Introduction

Las Vegas is often referred to as the Entertainment Capital of the World. However, hundreds of thousands of people also travel to Las Vegas every year to attend conventions and seminars.

Inside a small meeting room, located in a casino on the Vegas Strip, about 30 people gathered together for one such seminar. In the audience that day were several self-made millionaires, successful authors, motivational speakers, entrepreneurs, business owners and one cop who felt very much out of place.

Each of us had to stand before the group, introduce ourselves and explain why we were attending the seminar. I sat toward the back of the room and listened intently while the others stood up and spoke of their successful businesses and their future goals. As my time to speak approached, I became more aware how out of place I felt.

Most police officers will tell you they would rather chase an armed bank robber down a dark alley than to speak in front of a room full of strangers. I happen to enjoy doing both. I've had my share of chasing bad guys in my law enforcement career and I have also stood before groups of strangers speaking out on the dangers of drugs. But on that day, I was looking for the armed bank robber so I could bolt from the room!

When it was my turn, I stood up and talked about my personal experiences as a police officer and narcotics detective that have allowed me to see the tremendous impact drugs have on families and our communities. Educating people about the dangers of life-destroying drugs is my passion. I had traveled all over the country speaking and teaching about drugs, and I had been a guest on several national television shows including *The Oprah Winfrey Show*. But I wanted to reach more people and do more to prevent drug use and substance abuse.

INVOLVED: Parents' Connection to Drug Prevention

As I finished speaking a gentleman raised his hand and asked, "What would you tell a father who has spent more than a million dollars trying to keep his daughter from using drugs?" He went on to explain his daughter began using prescription drugs in medical school in an effort to pull all nighters studying. She graduated from med school with plans to become an anesthesiologist, but by that time her drug use had escalated into an addiction. This father now lives every day with fear that the next phone call will be the one where he learns his daughter is dead from a drug overdose or that she has accidentally killed a patient. The situation has become so intense he wasn't sure his 30-plus-years of marriage would be intact when he got home from the seminar. As the man described his situation, I could see the anxiety in his face and the pain in his eyes. His voice shifted between anger and sorrow. His question to me was more of a desperate plea as he searched for magical insights or words of wisdom that might make his nightmare disappear.

I stood for a moment in sadness. What do you tell a parent who has a child struggling with addiction? I knew nothing I said at that moment would change things for him or for his family. I replied; "I wish I had a magic wand to wave and take away your family's pain and your daughter's addiction. But there is no such thing. I know we can't give up on loved ones who struggle with addiction, and we must hold out hope for recovery one day. The only thing I can do is share with others what I have learned about the dangers of drugs and the impact drug use has on families and on all of us. The reason I am here today is because I am tired of seeing pain like yours. And the only way to stop the pain is for me to do what I can to prevent drug use before it ever starts."

During the next break, a married couple attending the seminar asked if my wife and I could join them for dinner. As we sat around the table that evening, they shared their personal story. It was this life-changing event that occurred when they were teenagers that fueled their passion to reach out to teens. Their message started inside one small classroom more than 20 years ago and continues to be repeated in schools across the country to this very day. Their workshops, assemblies and books for both parents and teens have touched millions of lives. The positive response from that message that started so many years ago was now stirring another passion – drug prevention.

Introduction

The invitation to dinner that night from Chuck and Marilyn Morris resulted in our writing this book. Marilyn and I share the same passion – to keep your child drug-free. And we hope what started that night around a small dinner table in a Las Vegas restaurant will alter attitudes in hundreds of schools and impact thousands of families. But we need your help. It's you as a parent and your *involvement* in your child's life that holds the key to drug prevention.

Our goal is that the insights you gain through reading *Involved* will empower you to become your child's connection to drug prevention.

Chapter 1

Reality Check

"There's no way my child would do drugs.
She's too intelligent to do something that stupid"

Those were the words spoken by a father 20 years ago referring to his daughter. Since that time, he has spent over a million dollars trying to help her overcome her addiction to drugs.

"I can't image my child trying drugs. He's just not the type.
But even if he did try it once or twice,
I don't think a little experimenting will hurt anything."

Those were the words of a mother referring to her teenage son. Before he graduated from high school, he tried a little marijuana. Ten years later his wife took their two children and filed for a divorce because of his addiction to cocaine and his inability to hold down a job.

"I don't have to worry about my son using drugs.
He has several friends using the stuff and
he's always trying to get them to stop".

Unfortunately, this dad learned it's easier for a young person to be pulled down than to pull others up after his teenage son was found dead from a heroin overdose.

Things Aren't Always as They Appear

If you've ever driven through the Deep South, you've probably noticed a beautiful green vine growing wild beside the roads and throughout the fields. During the summer, the vines produce a colorful flower that has a fragrant aroma. The plant was originally a gift from Japan at America's 100th birthday celebration. Southerners were thrilled as the plant flourished in their terrain. Entrepreneurs found a variety of ways to prosper from the miracle vine, producing baskets, paper and jellies. It even provided an inexpensive way to feed livestock and prevent erosion.

But today, Kudzu is a living nightmare as it climbs, chokes and destroys everything in its path. It now covers seven million acres, and each individual vine grows as much as 60 feet a year. This voracious, but innocent-looking plant, devours everything in its path, including trees, power lines, billboards, houses, parked cars and farm equipment.

The good news is horticulturalists have finally found a few herbicides that will actually kill the vine. The bad news is it takes years of continuous work to eradicate each and every plant. So those who don't want Kudzu consuming their yards, neighborhoods, fields and farmlands must be diligent in their determination to protect their property.

The drug problem in America is similar to the Kudzu problem of the Deep South. Like Kudzu, most drugs have been transported to America from other countries. Heroin comes from Mexico and areas in the Middle East and Asia. Cocaine is smuggled in from Columbia, Bolivia, and Peru. Ecstasy originated in Germany in the early 1900's, but now comes primarily from the Netherlands. And some drugs, such as methamphetamine and marijuana, are now home grown as drug-trafficking organizations increasingly grow and manufacture the drugs in the United States. But regardless of origin, all drugs have acclimated nicely in America.

> **Although the United States is home to only five percent of the world's population, we buy and consume 60 percent of the world's supply of illicit drugs.**[1]

Drugs are no respecter of persons or classes. They impact the lives of those living in urban poverty, middle-class suburbia and upper-class McMansions. Drugs have infiltrated our nation, and no community is untouched. Drugs arouse the curiosity of thrill seekers and risk takers who long for their first high or their next high. Some use drugs to bolster self confidence, while others use it to escape the pain of everyday life. In the same way Kudzu consumes everything in its path, drug use in a community spreads like the common cold. And what appears harmless one day can choke the life out of a family the next. Neither drugs nor Kudzu will be easily eliminated. Their roots are deep and their hold tenacious.

Money is the driving force behind these pills, powders and weeds. Drug cartels make billions worldwide, while "Mom and Pop" operations ply their trade in our neighborhoods for a piece of the financial action. In fact, it's possible your next-door neighbor is growing illegal weeds in his basement. The couple living behind you may be "cooking" methamphetamine in their kitchen to sell to neighborhood kids. Devastated lives and broken families? No concern of these people. It's all about the money.

The Good News!

Tucked away between cover stories and back-page editorials about teen drug usage is some good news. Even though teen drug use over the past 30 years resembles the ups and downs of a roller coaster, the good news is the overall, illegal drug use among American teens is presently on a downward slope. The question is – what's around the bend? Will the trend continue downward or is an upward climb on the horizon?

The University of Michigan's continuing research, *Monitoring the Future,* has questioned high school students since 1975 about their drug use. The following graph depicts the results of twelfth graders who have used illicit drugs at least once in their lifetime. (Note: The graph includes illicit drugs such as marijuana, cocaine, heroin and LSD. It does not include alcohol, tobacco or inhalants.)

INVOLVED: Parents' Connection to Drug Prevention

Monitoring the Future
National Results on Adolescent Drug Use[2]

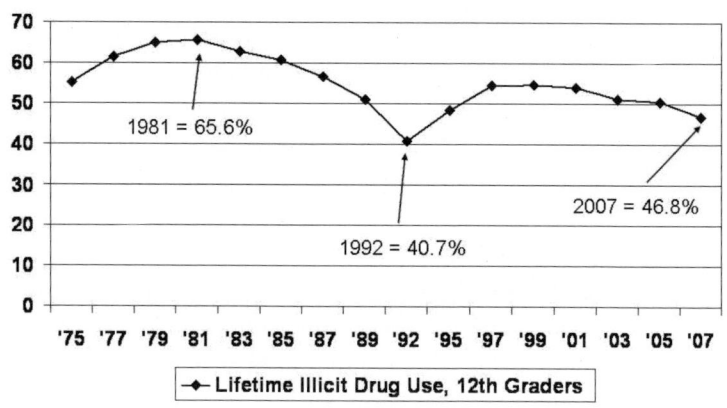

Okay, so maybe it's difficult to get excited over the fact that just under half of today's high school seniors have used marijuana, cocaine, heroin and/or LSD. But the point is, we *are* moving in the right direction!

One of the leading reasons fewer students turn to drugs today is because of parents like you. When parents diligently work to educate their children about the dangers of drugs, their children tend to listen and respond favorably. However, it is important this downward trend doesn't lull us into complacency.

Numerous factors have resulted in the significant shift in drug use among America's youth in the past few decades. Topping the list are pop culture and the media. Take another look at the dates on the time line and see if you can associate events that might have contributed to the increase or decrease in drug use regarding:

- Society's tolerance toward drug use vs. intolerance
- Prominent role models' and political figures' casual admission of use vs. a strong stance against drug use
- Relaxation of penalties for possession or use vs. strict and severe penalties against possession or use

Not My Child

The most uninformed statement a parent can make is, "Not my child," or "Not in my neighborhood." These words indicate a naiveté that runs counter to the facts. However, such parents are not alone. Studies by The Partnership for a Drug-Free America indicate how out of touch many parents are.

- *Four* percent of parents believe their teen has tried a non-prescription cold or cough medicine to get high.

  Ten percent of teens say they have gotten high with over-the-counter cold and cough medicines.

- *Five* percent of parents believe their teens have gotten high on prescription medicine that was not prescribed by their doctor.

  Nineteen percent of teens have used another person's medication to get high.[3]

- *Five* percent of parents believe their teen has used inhalants such as glue to get high.

  Twenty percent of teens say they have done this.[4]

- *Twenty-one* percent of parents believe their teen has friends who use marijuana.

  But *fifty-nine* percent of teens have at least one friend who uses marijuana[5]

- *Nineteen* percent of parents believe their teen has tried marijuana.

  But *thirty-seven* percent of teens have smoked marijuana at least once.[6]

It's a natural instinct to believe our children are inherently good, and it's hard for parents to believe their kids would ever try drugs. As a police officer, I (Todd) have had parents tell me many times, "not my kid," despite overwhelming evidence to the contrary.

However, we all need to wake up, wipe the sleep of deception from our eyes and face the fact that even good kids from good homes use drugs.

INVOLVED: Parents' Connection to Drug Prevention

Parents who believe drugs are not in their community are sadly and dangerously mistaken. The fact is the majority of our high school students and a large number of our middle school students attend schools where drugs are used, kept and/or sold. Each year millions of 12- to 17-year-olds experiment with tobacco, alcohol, marijuana or some other illicit drug for the first time.

Perhaps you are one of those adults who think a little experimentation is harmless and is just part of being a kid. If that's the case, then consider the following statistics:

- Of all the students who have tried cigarettes, nearly 90 percent (over 2 million) are still smoking in the twelfth grade.

- Of all the students who have gotten drunk, more than 80 percent (over 2 million) are still getting drunk in the twelfth grade.

- Of all the students who have tried marijuana, 75 percent (about 1.4 million) are still using it in twelfth grade.[7]

As you continue to turn the pages of this book, you will learn the younger a person is when he begins to use tobacco, alcohol and other drugs the greater the chance he will find himself drowning in a lifelong addiction – a nightmare your family does not want to experience.

Facing the Truth

It took years for Southerners to comprehend the impact of the Kudzu vine on their homeland. It was easy for residents to sit back and not give the plant a second thought until one day it appeared in their own yards.

The question is, how long will it take for Americans to wake up and realize what drugs are doing to our children, our homes, our schools and our communities? Drugs have already found their way onto our children's school buses and their classrooms, as well as their Friday-night parties and sleepovers. Parents blame the schools and teachers blame the parents. The finger-pointing must stop as we all take an active role in addressing and solving this epidemic. Law enforcement is doing all they can to combat drugs, but we will never arrest our way out of the problem.

But with *dedication* and *education*, attitudes about drug use can be changed. If we continue providing good information, today's youth are capable of making good choices!

Parents Make a Difference

It's been proven that when a parent prepares a child to fully comprehend the risk of using drugs, that child's potential of using drugs drops significantly. Your involvement in educating your children about drugs can make a tremendous difference in their future! For example:

1. Young people who learn about the risk of drugs from their parents are 50 percent less likely to try drugs than children who didn't get drug information from their parents.[8]

2. Over two-thirds of teens ages 13 to 17 say upsetting their parents or losing the respect of family and friends is one of the main reasons they don't use drugs.[9]

Taking Time to Connect

Never in history has a generation of children come from so much wealth and been given such an abundance of materialistic *stuff* as today's American young people. However, many of these young people are starved, not for food, but for their parent's love, attention and acceptance. More and more parents find there just aren't enough hours in the day to make enough money to buy all the *stuff* they want and have quality time left over to invest in their children. Of course, there's no guarantee, even with a stay-at-home-parent, the children will receive the attention they crave and deserve.

(Marilyn's Story) Like most mothers of the '50's and '60's, my mother was a hardworking, stay-at-home mom. With five people in my family, just keeping up with the laundry was a monumental task, especially since we didn't have a clothes dryer. So not only did my

mother wash the clothes, she hung each individual piece on the line to dry. She then brought the clothes back inside and starched the appropriate pieces; and I'm not talking spray starch.

My most vivid memory of my mother was of her standing in the kitchen ironing. It was a never-ending job. When I was about five, I remember Mom looking up from the ironing board and saying, "Marilyn, one of these days I'm going to stop my housework, and we're going to play."

I remember those words as if it were yesterday. I spent a lot of time thinking about what we might do when she made the big announcement, "Okay, let's play." Would I want to play dolls or maybe we'd play *Shoots and Ladders*. It really didn't matter what we did. Just spending time with my mother, laughing and having fun, would be wonderful.

Weeks turned into months. Months turned into years. Then one day I was an adult and realized – Mom never did stop her housework long enough to play with me. When I think back to my childhood, I remember our house as always being orderly. Our clothes were always clean and neatly pressed. Dinner was always on the table at the appropriate time, but I have absolutely no recollection of ever playing with my mother.

Today, our society is filled with parents who are outstanding providers of materialistic things. Homes are neat, clean and full of beautiful furnishings. Garages are filled with expensive cars. Children have swimming pools, trampolines, computers, cell phones and jet skis. But the one thing these children are lacking is a relationship with their parents.

> **Children who are *NOT* connected to and regularly monitored by their parents are four times more likely to use drugs.**[10]

(Todd's Story) I was three when my parents divorced. My mother worked long hours to support our family and raise four children as a single mom. She sacrificed her own happiness to provide for her children. As much as she would have wanted to spend quality

time with us, there just weren't enough hours in the day for that to happen.

My dad was often in another state and had little contact with our family. It seemed like years would go by without a call or a birthday card from him. It crushed me to see my friends and their fathers at school. I remember growing up and listening to the Harry Chapin song, "Cat's in the Cradle," and singing the lyrics:

> A child arrived just the other day,
> He came to the world in the usual way.
> But there were planes to catch, and bills to pay.
> He learned to walk while I was away.
> And he was talking 'fore I knew it, and as he grew,
> He'd say, "I'm gonna be like you, dad.
> You know I'm gonna be like you."
>
> Chorus: And the cat's in the cradle and the silver spoon,
> Little boy blue and the man in the moon.
> "When you coming home, dad?" "I don't know when,
> But we'll get together then.
> You know we'll have a good time then…"

If you remember the song, then you know it concludes with the father as an old man, calling his grown-up son and expressing a desire to spend some time together. The son replies,

> "… I'd love to, dad, if I could find the time.
> You see, my new job's a hassle, and the kid's got the flu,
> But it's sure nice talking to you, dad.
> It's been sure nice talking to you."
> And as I hung up the phone, it occurred to me,
> He'd grown up just like me.
> My boy was just like me.
>
> Chorus: And the cat's in the cradle and the silver spoon,
> Little boy blue and the man in the moon.
> "When you coming home, son?" "I don't know when,
> But we'll get together then, dad.
> You know we'll have a good time then."

Do the lyrics of that song move you as you think about the relationship with your parents? What about the time you spend with your children?

INVOLVED: Parents' Connection to Drug Prevention

Ironically, my life followed the lyrics of that song all too closely. In the last couple years of my dad's life, it was hard for me to find time for him. The years apart when I was growing up left us with nothing in common and there was little to talk about. After his death, I thought of so many things I wished I had asked him. I realize now how the distance between us in the latter years must have broken his heart, just as mine had been broken years before.

My two older sons were six and eight when their mother and I divorced. Suddenly I was face-to-face with the reality of history repeating itself. Going from a full-time parent to part-time parent opened my eyes to the importance of quality time with my sons. I often wonder: Had I not divorced, would I have continued to take my relationship with my sons for granted?

I made the decision to make changes and become more *involved* with their daily lives. During their elementary school days, I volunteered in their class as often as my work schedule would permit. During reading week, I read to their class. On field day, I coached as the kids competed against other classmates. Not only did I get great enjoyment in participating with my own kids, it was such a reward to receive the hand-made thank-you cards from the other children.

I know it's hard for many working parents to volunteer during the day. I was fortunate to have that opportunity. However, taking one vacation day to spend time at school with your child helps create a lifelong memory.

As great as it was to spend occasional time with my sons during the school day, we had no real hobbies we could enjoy together as they grew older. I had introduced them to sports, karate and music, but neither of the boys took a liking to any of them.

I knew the boys would soon develop their own interests, and I would be competing with their friends for time on the weekends. I was afraid of hearing them say they didn't have time for me. We needed something to keep us connected, and I found it in paintball. For Christmas one year I purchased all the gear we needed, including a couple of extra set-ups for their friends. We spent a few weekends a month playing, and it was some of the most fun I have ever had with them. But as they have reached high school, found their own interests and manage more of their own time, staying involved requires a constant commitment on my part.

My new wife and I have two more sons. That's right! I have four sons! I realize what a different dad I am today than I was a few years ago with my first two sons. My mistakes of the past are my motivator to work even harder at staying connected with my younger sons.

Believe me, I am not the perfect parent. I still find myself saying more times than I would like, "not now," or, "maybe later." It takes a concentrated effort not to fall in the rut of the daily grind and overlook spending time with our children.

The point is, as a parent, there is absolutely nothing more valuable you can give your child than time. When you give time, you give yourself. And what follows is a connection that results in love, security and acceptance.

What to Expect From This Book

While there are no easy solutions or guarantees in life, this book provides three important steps to help you protect your child from drugs.

Step #1: *Involved* **explains why you and your children should be concerned about the drug problems in America.**

You don't have to have a family member using drugs to be affected by drugs. In fact, whether you know it or not, illegal drugs are affecting you and your family every single day in ways you have probably never considered. Once you understand the problems drugs are causing, you will be able to pass that information on to your children, thus empowering them to become part of the solution and not part of the problem.

Step #2: *Involved* **educates you about the drug scene and commonly abused drugs.**

As a parent, you fit into one of three categories:

(1) You never did drugs.

(2) You experimented with them a little.

(3) You've been there, done that and got the T-shirt.

No matter which category you fit into, this book will help you understand the importance of educating yourself about drugs. Even if you used drugs years ago, you're probably not up on today's terms and trends that are crucial warning signs of drug use. For example, would you be concerned if you saw the numbers **420** or the word **tina** written on your child's book cover? You should be! Do you know what it means if someone asks, **"Are you rolling?"** After you read this book you will.

The more knowledge you have the better. After all, it's far easier for a child to get away with using drugs when Mom and Dad are clueless about today's drug scene, drug paraphernalia and the warning signs of drug use. If your child was offered drugs, wouldn't it be great if his response was, "No, thanks! My parents know way too much about drugs. If I started using, they'd know!"

Maybe you're one of those who believe that because you smoked a little weed in high school or tried a few lines of coke in college and nothing bad happened to you, your child's experimentation is no big deal. After all, you grew out of it; and so can he. Unfortunately, no one ever plans on becoming addicted or overdosing on drugs. Yet millions of Americans suffer from drug addictions and thousands die each year. Is that a gamble you're willing to take with your child's life?

Step #3: Each chapter in *Involved* provides you with creative ideas on how to protect your child from drugs.

As already stated, there is no magic formula to guarantee your child will avoid the drug scene. However, there are many things you can do to greatly reduce the risk. At the conclusion of each chapter is a section entitled ***The Parent Connection to Drug Prevention.*** It's packed with creative ideas to help you prepare your children for the realities of life and protect them from the drug scene.

The Parent Connection

Ideas to Help You Protect Your Child From Drugs

Making the Connection

When your child was a baby, it was easy to stay connected. Considering babies are totally dependent upon the adults in their lives, that connection was easy to maintain. But now that your child is gaining independence, it's easy to become disconnected.

DON'T LET IT HAPPEN!

It's the disconnected children – the ones who are lonely and depressed – who are far more likely to turn to drugs and alcohol. Just as a light bulb goes dark when it's removed from the lamp, so the light inside a child quickly fades when he is not connected to his parents.

This brings us to the first tip on the Parent Connection to drug prevention:

Tip # 1 on DRUG PREVENTION

Stay Connected with Your Child.

 **TRY THIS TIP!**

One Simple Thing Can Make a BIG Difference!

What if I told you there was one simple thing you can do that will improve your child's grades and college ambition. Would you be interested in knowing what that one thing is? And what if I told you this one thing will also lower your child's chance of:

- Lying to you by 15 percent
- Smoking by 26 percent
- Being suspended from school by 29 percent
- Fighting by 29 percent
- Getting involved in sex by 37 percent
- Drinking alcohol by 41 percent
- Using marijuana by 41 percent
- Attempting suicide by 71 percent

So do I have your undivided attention? The one thing is…

Eat Dinner with Your Teen at Least Five Nights a Week.[11]

Families who make it a priority to slow down the chaotic rat race of life for 30 to 40 minutes a day while they eat dinner together build strong connections with those sitting around the table. Talking, laughing and sharing life over a meal builds lifelong bonds and says, "You are important to me!"

Exploring Ways to Stay Connected

With just a little effort, you can find endless ways to stay *involved* with your child. For younger children, simply reading a book or blowing bubbles together is a great way to stay connected. But as your children get older, you may have to step out of your comfort zone to find creative ways to stay connected. Although video games may consume too much time for many kids, they are a large part of today's culture. I (Todd) have had my own difficulty in acknowledging the usefulness of video games! Yet even today's military understands the importance of high-tech games, and they incorporate video-game-style simulators for real military training.

A wide variety of games allow for multiple players. Playing a video game with your teen allows you to acknowledge their interests while sharing some laughs and excitement. Most game systems have suitable games the entire family can enjoy. I recently broke down and purchased a game system which allows for interactive play. A sensor monitors the movement of the hand controllers, which then controls the actions on the screen. My sons who don't like real sports will play an hour of video game sports with me. The interactive action of the game actually provides some aerobic exercise as well!

Here are more ways you and your child can stay connected.

At Home
- Find a hobby to share with your child
    - collect baseball cards, coins or stamps
    - restore an old car, plant a garden, make jewelry, reupholster furniture, build a birdhouse
- Take a class together – computers, photography, painting, drawing, pottery, dancing, cooking, yoga
- Go camping, fishing or rock climbing together
- Play laser tag or go-kart racing
- Play golf, go to a driving range or play miniature golf
- Go to concerts or sporting events together
- Play tennis or shoot some baskets together
- Go ice skating, roller skating or ride bikes
- Go out to dinner and have dessert first
- Do a jig-saw puzzle together
- Take a Surprise Trip! – Plan an overnight or weekend family trip to see a distant relative. Once the car is packed and you're on the road, announce you're actually going to a hotel with a great indoor pool or next to an amusement park
- Work on projects together around the house
  - paint the fence, rake leaves, build a tree house
- Have a garage sale and buy something the entire family wants with the proceeds
- Go on ice cream or donut runs together late at night
- Watch a late night movie and eat popcorn together

At School (This includes dads)
- Volunteer at your child's school - homeroom mom or dad, office assistant, tutor, teacher's aide
- Chaperon field trips
- Attend your child's sporting events, school plays, choir or band concerts

Community Service
You and your child can:
- Cook a meal together for a sick friend or relative
- Shovel snow for an elderly couple
- Offer your services to baby sit for a young couple who need a night out
- Volunteer your time at a homeless shelter
- Have a garage sale and give the proceeds to a needy family

Other Ways to Stay Connected
- Put a note in your child's lunch box or under her pillow expressing your love and appreciation.
- If you can't be home before your children go to bed, stop what you're doing long enough to talk to them on the phone and see how their day went.
- Give each of your children a minimum of 15 minutes of one-on-one, eye-to-eye attention every single day – more on the weekend.

TRY THIS IDEA!

Happy Memory Moments

As a means of staying connected with your child, get in the habit of asking the following question every Sunday evening as a new week begins:

Reality Check

What was your favorite memory this past week?

As your child shares his Happy Memory Moment each week, you can obtain valuable insights about what makes him happy, his attitudes on life and overall well-being. You can also use this as a means to measure your success as a parent.

No doubt many, perhaps even most, of your child's Happy Memory Moments will be focused on school activities or things he did with his friends. The older he gets the more likely this will be the case, and there's nothing wrong with that. After all, school and best friends make up a large portion of your child's life. But if you are never or seldom included in his Happy Memory Moments, this could be an indication you aren't spending enough quality time with him.

But don't think you're going to have to pack up the family and fly to California or Florida for a trip to Disney to be included in your child's Happy Memory Moments. Remember, I (Marilyn) would have been thrilled had my mother simply turned the iron off for 30 minutes and said, "Let's play!"

A Happy Memory Moment may consist of something as simple as making cookies with your 8-year-old, riding bikes with your 10-year-old, shooting baskets with your 14-year-old or making a donut run at midnight with your 16-year-old.

You can expand this idea of *Happy Memory Moments* by asking your child at the end of each month: *What was your favorite memory of this month?* And a great question for New Years Eve each year would be: *What was your favorite Happy Memory of the year?* You might want to secretly record your child's Happy Memory of each year and share these at a special time later in his life – perhaps his 18th or 21st birthday or at his college graduation party or at the rehearsal dinner for his wedding. Many years from now, your grandchildren might enjoy hearing you read about their mother or father's Happy Memory Moment List.

Strive to make lots of Happy Memory Moments
with your children that can be cherished for a lifetime!

References

[1] OHS – Health and Safety Services, Inc., "What Every Employer Should Know about Drug-Abuse in the Workplace," 2004.
[2] National Institute on Drug Abuse. *Monitoring the Future National Results on Adolescent Drug Use: Overview of Key Findings 2007*, April 2008.
[3] The Partnership for a Drug Free America, *The Partnership Attitude Tracking Study*, 2005.
[4] The Partnership for a Drug-Free America, *Teens and Inhalant Abuse*, 2006.
[5] The Partnership for a Drug-Free America, *Partnership Attitude Tracking Study*, 2004.
[6] The Partnership for a Drug Free America, *The Partnership Attitude Tracking Study*, 2005.
[7] The National Center on Addiction and Substance Abuse (CASA), *The Malignant Neglect: Substance Abuse & America's Schools*, 2001.
[8] Partnership for a Drug-Free America, *Partnership Attitude Tracking Study*, 2003.
[9] Partnership for a Drug-Free America, *Partnership Attitude Tracking Study*, 2005.
[10] Metzler, Rusby, & Biglan, Oregon Research Institute, Eugene, 1999, Community Builders for Success: Monitoring After School Activities.
[11] US Council of Economic Advisors, "Teens and Their Parents in the 21st Century: An Examination of Trends in Teen Behavior and the Role of Parental Involvement," Economic Advisors White Paper, May 2000. www.clinton3.nara.gov/WH/EOP/CEA/html/Teens_Paper_Final.pdf

Chapter 2

The Importance of a Dream

Todd's Story

Can you remember someone coming up to you and saying, "Do you want to try this?"

I remember the day very well. I was a freshman in high school. It was a rainy day, and I was waiting at a bus stop trying to stay dry. There were a bunch of older kids, and they were all passing around a marijuana cigarette. One of the older kids looked at me and said, "You want to try it, kid?"

I looked at him and said without hesitation, "No. When I grow up I want to be a police officer."

He laughed at me and said, "Don't fool yourself. Cops smoke pot, too."

"Not this one," I replied. And that was my introduction to drugs – that first temptation.

At that point, my parents had never talked to me about drugs. But I remembered *Officer Friendly* who had come to my elementary school years before and talked to my class about drugs being dangerous. I remembered how that police officer took his time to personally encourage me, and he made me feel important. For a young boy without a father around, just those few minutes had a profound impact on my life. But something else also caused me to say no to drugs as I stood at the bus stop that rainy day. It was a dream – one that was ingrained deep within me.

The next time I came into contact with drugs was when I was 19. I was in the military and had come home on leave to see my family.

INVOLVED: Parents' Connection to Drug Prevention

My brother was six years older than I and had his own place. My mother had a tendency to worry about him because he was a diabetic, and she hadn't heard from him in a few days. She asked me to go to his apartment and bring him to the house. When I got to his place, it looked deserted. Newspapers were piled up in front, and there were several fliers in the door. I knocked, but no one answered. I feared my brother was inside and needed help, so I knocked the door down. It wasn't a very sturdy door, and it opened fairly easily. Thankfully, my brother wasn't inside the house. Unfortunately, I saw what was – burnt aluminum foil, syringes and drug residue.

That was my first glimpse of what drugs can do to a family. A lot of parents and siblings know exactly what I'm talking about. Learning a loved one is using drugs and feeling the helplessness of not being able to help that person overcome the addiction destroying his life is frustrating and painful.

I only saw my brother a handful of times during the fifteen or so years after that day. But I never forgot what I saw in his apartment. My time in the military and later living in different parts of the country left little chance to see each other. Deep inside I knew it was more than distance keeping us apart. My brother was addicted to drugs, and he intentionally stayed away from the family – partly out of shame and partly to protect us from the pain of seeing him battle his addiction. But I never stopped wanting to help him; and if I couldn't help him, maybe I could help others.

A Dream Come True

As I was growing up, I dreamed of being an undercover narcotics officer. Of course, television and the media rarely portray the image of a narc in a positive light. But I believed I could make a difference. I chose to follow that dream in Las Vegas, Nevada.

I spent five years as a uniformed police officer patrolling the inner-city neighborhoods. In the evenings the crack dealers stood on the corner selling their wares. As the night gave way to day, children waiting for the school bus replaced them. I saw kids playing in parks while addicts got their fix in the nearby alley. I saw first-hand the toll drugs took on these neighborhoods. I saw things most people never dream of or think exists in their own community; but no matter where you live, they exist. Not only do they exist, they flourish.

When you think of a drug addict, what image comes to your mind? Like most, you probably visualize the *crack head* or *junkie* you've seen on TV or passed by when you accidentally drove through one of *those* neighborhoods. When I became a narcotics detective, I thought I knew it all. I saw what happened in my school, in my own family and on the street. But I was awakened to a whole new world. The sobering reality is, the true image of an addict is a mother, a father, brother, sister, son and daughter. And I'm not just talking about those in the inner city. I'm talking about teachers, police officers, doctors, lawyers and politicians who live in middle- and upper-class neighborhoods. You don't usually see these folks in the news.

I remember when I first started seeing a drug on the street known as ecstasy. I had never heard of it. It had gained popularity in the early 80's but had faded away for almost fifteen years. But when it resurfaced on the streets of Las Vegas, it hit with a vengeance. It was showing up primarily in nightclubs with the 20-something age group. Then it began to filter down into the hands of younger kids as well.

I was working undercover and socializing with those who were selling and using the drug. I was hearing first-hand the wonderful stories about how great ecstasy was and about the unbelievable way it made users feel. Everyone kept marveling how there were no negative side effects. Ecstasy appeared to be the wonder drug of the day!

It's hard to admit, but for the first time in my life I was tempted. I remember thinking to myself, "What's wrong with me? I have NEVER been tempted to try a drug. Now here I am, almost 10 years on the police force with a family, and I am actually curious to see what it would be like to try one of those little pills." Then I thought to myself, "If I weren't where I am today, if I didn't have so much to lose, if I wasn't a police officer with a family, this is the one drug I think I might try."

That temptation scared me. To come that close. To be so tempted. Then my thoughts turned back to the ninth grade, standing at the bus stop on that rainy day when I turned down my first invitation to try drugs. I could still hear that kid laugh when I told him I was going to be a policeman. Then, as if he were standing right beside me,

I could hear his reply echo in my mind, "Don't fool yourself, cops smoke pot too."

"Not this one," I replied . . . not this one . . . not this one!

Wow! If a well-educated police officer can be tempted, what must it be like to be a 14- or 15-year-old kid today who believes he has nothing to lose? Someone hands him this powerful little pill, which will make him feel *WONDERFUL* as it erases away all the cares of the world. What's going to stop him?

It was that experience and that very question that prompted me to walk out of my undercover world and devote my life to educating teens, parents and families about the impact drugs have on our everyday lives. Drugs impacts each of us every day, but most people go about their daily lives oblivious to the problems drugs are causing our society. Unfortunately, in my career, I've seen families torn apart by drug use; and I've met dozens of parents who've lost children because of drugs. But it goes far beyond that. We are all paying a tremendous price for drugs, and few recognize the destruction.

And so it's my hope this book opens up a world most people know very little about. A world many don't even know exists. I believe this book will help parents and families experience what I see day after day.

Dreaming of a Bright Future

Think back to what you just read. The one thing that kept Todd from stumbling and trying drugs was his determination to fulfill his childhood dream of becoming a police officer. In the ninth grade, he already knew where he was going, what he wanted to do; and he wasn't going to let anyone take his dream away from him.

Question

Does your child have a dream, something he or she is passionately working toward?

Are you helping your child identify and reach that dream?

The Importance of a Dream

Marilyn's Story

Now that you've heard Todd's story, let me tell you mine. If you've read my parent book, *ABC's of the Birds and Bees for Parents of Toddlers to Teens* or my student book, *Teens Sex and Choices* then you know I too had a childhood dream of becoming someone special. As early as 12 years old, I knew I wanted to be a professional tennis player.

Throughout my junior high and high school years, I played in tennis tournaments across Texas. I often dreamed of the day I would walk across the stage at my high school graduation, and those in the audience would turn to one another and whisper, "She's the tennis player."

But there was a major difference in my dream and Todd's dream. I never shared my dream with another living soul. Not one person on the face of the earth knew I wanted to get a scholarship to Trinity University in San Antonio and then make my way onto the professional tennis circuit. Oh sure, all my family and friends knew I spent all my time on the tennis courts, but no one knew I had my future all mapped out in great detail.

When I was 15-years-old, a sophomore in high school, I went on a blind date with a young man. This guy was a football player, a member of the student council and a straight-A student. From that first night, I knew there was something special about this guy. Every time he took me in his arms my heart melted. By my junior year in high school, my passion for tennis was fading while my passion for romance was igniting. With no accountability partners or mentors by my side, I was left alone, struggling to decide what to do with the out-of-control feelings and urges I was experiencing. And since I had never shared my dream of being a professional tennis player with another living soul, there was no one questioning the sudden change in my attitude toward tennis. But at 16, it certainly was a lot more thrilling to focus my energy on a relationship with a guy than exhaust myself on the tennis courts in the hot Texas sun day after day.

It wasn't until the beginning of my senior year in high school that I awoke to the reality of what I had done and the mistake I had made. Chuck was now in college and had little time for me. It was obvious our relationship was coming to an end. I was devastated. I also

INVOLVED: Parents' Connection to Drug Prevention

knew it was too late to do anything spectacular with tennis. Although I continued to play in tournaments across the state throughout high school, I hadn't brought home the first-place trophies necessary to gain recognition by leading universities. I knew I had blown any hope of receiving a scholarship. With my love life now coming to an end, I determined that if I worked hard enough and totally focused on my tennis game during my senior year, perhaps I could still make my way onto a college team somewhere.

That's about the time my world came crashing down around me. Just as I was trying to cope with the reality that the love of my life was losing interest in me and our relationship was coming to a close, I also became aware of an earth-shattering reality – I was pregnant. Over the next several weeks, my life became a shambles as Chuck and I walked through a living nightmare. I was 17 and he was 18. We were two really good kids from good homes. We had both been raised in the church. We had *never* caused our parents any trouble – and that was our biggest concern. How could we do this to our parents?

This was the fall of 1968. This sort of thing just didn't happen to good kids. Abortion was not legal and thus was not an option we even considered. And no respectable teenage girl at that time became a single mother. Therefore, we were left with only two options – place the baby for adoption or get married.

While Chuck may have wished he could have gotten out of this mess the easy way, he did exactly what was expected of any respectable young man back then – he married me. The wedding was on a Saturday evening over the Thanksgiving holidays.

I went back to school on Monday morning and shocked all my friends and teachers when I announced I was married. The rule back then was a girl could stay in school if she was married and/or pregnant, but she couldn't be involved in any extracurricular activities. That meant no school parties, no prom – and no tennis. Therefore, before I left school on that Monday afternoon, I cleaned out my locker in the tennis dressing room and walked away from my dream of becoming a professional tennis player once and for all.

In May I graduated with my 700 classmates. And just as I had once dreamed of, people did notice when I walked across the stage. But instead of whispering, "She's the tennis player," they were whispering, "She's the pregnant girl." You see, out of the 2,000

The Importance of a Dream

students at Monterey High School in Lubbock, Texas – only two of us went through the school year pregnant. *My, how times have changed!*

Many years have now come and gone. Surprisingly, the ending to my story is not the typical tragedy of most teenage marriages. I'm thrilled to tell you, Chuck and I are still married. We are also the proud parents of two beautiful daughters. Our first daughter was born on our seven-month wedding anniversary, and our second daughter was born three years later. Our daughters and their husbands have blessed us with five adorable grandchildren – three boys and two girls.

No, I never become a star tennis player, but my experiences did pave the way for another passion. Since the mid '80's, I have devoted my life to speaking to teenagers and sharing a message of sexual abstinence until marriage – a message I wish someone had shared with me back when I was growing up.

By the early 1990's the speaking engagements had become more than I could handle alone. So in 1993, Chuck and I founded an educational organization called Aim For Success, Inc. Since Chuck is a CPA, he easily stepped into the role of CFO and oversees the business side of the company while I head-up the speaking. Each year, my speaking staff and I provide around 2,000 presentations across the country. We have captivated, educated and entertained millions of teens, parents and educators through live presentations as well television and radio appearances.

My greatest desire is to impress upon you the importance of staying *involved* in your children's lives and empowering them to stay focused on a bright, exciting future. As you will see throughout this book, you really do hold the key to your child's success. While you cannot make choices for your children, you can provide the necessary information and support to help them stay on the straight and narrow path to make good choices about smoking, alcohol, drugs… and yes, even sex!

I hope my story also serves as a reminder that good things can eventually come from bad situations. I'm sure most adults who witnessed the mess Chuck and I were in those many years ago gave our marriage no chance of survival. And I must admit, there were rough times where the "D" word crossed my mind. But I can honestly say, Chuck is absolutely my very best friend; and we are having so much fun growing (dare I say) "old" together! And every time we look at our two daughters and their husbands and our five grandchildren we are reminded good things really can come from bad situations!

If you are struggling with a child who is rebellious or into drugs or other risky behaviors, please understand this doesn't mean there is no hope. No matter what your situation is right now, hang in there and strive to provide your children unconditional love and support – even when you don't support their choices. Encourage them with the endless possibilities of an amazing future when they *dream big!*

The Parent Connection

Ideas to Help You Protect Your Child From Drugs

Dreaming with Your Child

I (Marilyn) talked to a 38-year-old man this week who told me he was the quarterback of his high school football team and captain of both the football and baseball team. He made good grades, came from a good home, grew up in the church – yet he did drugs in high school and college. He said that although he knew all about the dangers of drugs, he never feared what they might do to him or his future. When I asked him why, he thought for a minute and said, "I guess because no one ever told me I was special or had potential. I just couldn't see I had anything to lose by doing drugs."

Let me ask you again:

> Does your child have a dream, something he or she is passionate about?

Are you helping your child reach for that dream?

I speak to teenagers in schools all across the country. I usually begin the program by asking the students what they want to do when they finish high school. Sixth graders are quick to raise their hands and respond. "I want to fly airplanes." "I want to be a professional football player." "I want to be a fashion designer." "I want to be a marine biologist."

But when I ask juniors and seniors the same question, the majority of them just look at me with a blank stare. Few are thinking farther than Friday night's party. The seniors may know there are exactly 48 days until graduation, but they have no clue what they will do after they finish high school.

That's why it's taking so many kids five or more years to finish college. They enter college without dreams and goals. They spend the first two to three years wandering aimlessly, having no idea what they want to do with their lives. Then, after a few years, they're tired of school and tend to settle on whatever will allow them to get out of college in the shortest amount of time.

However, not all students are like that. In nearly all high schools there are those few students, perhaps only a handful, who seem to know exactly where they are going. These students are determined that nothing is going to get in their way. And although they might shift from one dream to another, they always seem to always have a long-term plan. In ten years from now, the majority of those students will still be focused and have their lives together.

Supporting and encouraging your child's dream does more than help him achieve his goals. It also allows the two of you a chance to form a lasting bond. Then, when the pressures of life come around and someone says to him, "Hey, kid, you want to try this little pill? It'll make you feel wonderful," he's far more likely to say *NO* than the young person who has no idea where he's headed in life with no purpose or direction, no one who believes in him and cares enough to dream with him. Parents who are plugged into their child's daily life are far more likely to discern when their child is losing focus of their dream. Such parents are in a far better position to ascertain what is causing the distraction and open a dialogue about what is happening.

Which one is your child – the one with a life full of dreams and goals or the one with no idea where he's going? This book is filled with creative ideas that will help you encourage your child to reach for the stars and stay focused on dreams and goals.

This brings us to the second tip on the Parent Connection to Drug Prevention:

Tip #2 on DRUG PREVENTION

Dream with Your Child about a Bright Future.

TRY THESE TIPS

Dream a Little Dream with Me!

If your children are going to be focused on a dream in life, then you need to be dreaming with them on a daily basis about a bright, wonderful future. Sit down with each of your children, ages 5 through 18, and ask them what they want to be when they grow-up. If their answer is, "I don't know," give them one week to come up with an answer. Encourage them to think about the things they like to do. After all, it's difficult to be successful in life if you aren't doing what you enjoy! Within a week, make sure each of your children have declared their dream.

Then, no matter what your child comes up with, be excited and provide encouragement. Remember, you're just having fun dreaming together right now; and the sky is the limit. To add to the excitement, make a sign proclaiming your child's dream. "Will is going to be a *surgeon!* Riley is going into the *military!* Sarah is going to be a *veterinarian!* Reid is going to be a *professional basketball player! Katie* is going to be a *teacher!*" Then post their dreams on the refrigerator or bedroom doors. This will serve as a constant reminder that each of your children has a dream!

Once your child has declared what the dream is, keep running with it as long as your child continues to be excited about that dream. If he loses interest, give him a week to come up with a new dream. Remember, it's dangerous for a child to wander through life without a goal.

Perhaps I should interject a word of warning at this point. Some kids change dreams more often than they change their socks. That's okay. Be flexible and shift gears with each new dream. If you keep doing this long enough, one day you'll realize the dream hasn't changed in a long time, and one day that dream may become reality.

So let's say your 12-year-old daughter says she wants to be an actress. Remember, even if you hate the thought of her becoming an actress, this is *her* dream – not yours. Give her a chance to think through the pros and cons for a while. There's a good chance this dream will fade away and be replaced by something else. But if it doesn't fade, she might surprise you and be famous someday.

So now that she's established she wants to be an actress, you could start asking questions to stimulate her thoughts along that line. When you're driving to the grocery store, you could ask her to name her favorite actor. Then encourage her to research that person on the Internet and share with you what she learned. You might also want to watch the Biography Channel together and see what different movie stars had to go through to become successful. Few actors made it big without going through extremely difficult times.

When she gives a book report at school or has to recite poetry in English class, remind her that this is great preparation for becoming an actress. After all, if she follows through with her dream of becoming an actress, she's going to have to get comfortable speaking in public and memorizing long scripts. It might be at that point she determines she hates speaking in public, and being an actress isn't for her. So now you give her another week to come up with another dream.

Let's say your son, who's a sophomore in high school, tells you he wants to be a professional football player. Again, you might cringe at his response, knowing full well he doesn't have the makings of a professional football player – but keep your mouth shut. Let him come to that conclusion on his own. Remember, your job is to build him up – not tear him down. Besides, you might be wrong.

Start asking him questions that will force him to think about his dream. "What position would you like to play?" "Where would you like to go to college?" "What does it take to get on a college team?"

Then send him to the Internet and have him start researching universities and football scholarships, etc. Once he does his research, he might figure out there's no way he'd ever make a college team. But you can encourage him to have fun playing football in high school while he focuses on another dream for the future.

Let's say he decides he likes the thought of being a lawyer. You don't cringe this time. In fact, you really like the idea. Once again you start asking him questions, and you send him to the Internet to research what it takes to be a lawyer. After a few weeks of research, he realizes he needs to get more serious about his grades. The two of you start spending time together looking at different law schools on the Internet. You have a friend at work whose husband is an attorney, and

The Importance of a Dream

you invite them over for dinner. Your son takes this opportunity to ask questions. The attorney is impressed with your son's enthusiasm and invites him to sit through an up-coming trial. That summer he even gives your son some odd jobs to do around his law firm. By his junior year it's time to start visiting college campuses so that by his senior year he knows what he's going to major in as well as his top five choices in colleges.

Do you see what a difference this can make? He has a dream for his life. He's working toward making that dream a reality, and he has someone to share his dream with on a regular basis. And when he goes to a party on Saturday night and someone offers him a little pill that will ease life's inevitable bumps and bruises he has no problem saying, "No, thanks." Why? Because he doesn't need a pill to make him feel good. He already feels good about his life. He's focused on a bright future, and he knows someone believes in him – YOU!

Now here's a word of warning: Don't get upset if he announces his sophomore year in college that he wants to change his major from pre-law to computer science. Just let him share why he believes this would be a better fit. Remember, it's *his* dream – not yours! And don't look at the years you invested in him preparing to be a lawyer as a waste of time. It served its purpose. It gave him a dream. That dream caused his grades to improve, it allowed the two of you to grow closer, and it gave him a reason to say no to drugs and other risky behaviors.

It's also important to mention at this point that not all young people are cut out for college. That doesn't change anything. You can still dream on a daily basis of a bright future. For example, let's say your 16-year-old son's dream is to be an auto mechanic. The sign on the refrigerator or bedroom door should then proclaim, "Jack's going to be an *AUTO MECHANIC!*"

Perhaps one of the best things you can do is provide an engine for him to tear apart and rebuild or maybe locate an old car for him to restore. You can also encourage him to use his talents to help others. Perhaps there's an elderly couple or single mom on your block who could use an oil change or help in fixing a flat tire. Later, if he decides he wants to go into construction instead of becoming a mechanic, you are assured his days of rebuilding an engine or restoring the car served a great purpose. Not only did it keep him busy, it also kept him focused on a goal for life while providing invaluable knowledge about how machines work and how to repair them.

Short-Term Goals

Dreaming of a goal doesn't have to be just about the future. Short-term goals are also important! At the beginning of each school year it is wise to ask your child to determine two or three goals she would like to accomplish during the school year. Have her write the goals down so the two of you can track her progress. Perhaps one of her goals would be to save enough money to go to camp the following summer. The two of you could determine how much money she should save each month to reach her goal. Then every month or two talk about how she's doing in fulfilling her goal. If she begins to fall behind, don't hand her the money. Instead, talk about ideas that will enable her to catch up. Then continue to encourage her to succeed with her goal.

There are also short-term goals that can be fun for the entire family. For example, around Thanksgiving start planning, as a family, what you want to do for the upcoming holidays. You might consider hosting an open house. You and your children can have fun making the guest list, designing the invitations, decorating the house inside and out, and making all kinds of delicious candies and cookies. Help your children understand the joy of giving by providing gifts and food for family and friends, as well as for needy families.

Believe it or not, by doing all this, you're actually helping your children say no to drugs. Young people who feel connected to their family, who are busy, who feel important and see the value of life are far more likely to say no when someone asks if they want to get high.

Help your children stay high on life, so they won't feel the need to get high on drugs!

Chapter 3

Why Should You Care About Drug Abuse?

So what's the big deal about drugs? As long as your children don't use the stuff, why should you care what other people do with their lives? After all, this is a free country, right? Shouldn't each of us be able to make our own decisions about using drugs?

The reality is drugs affect each of us every day in our communities, in our homes, in our schools, in our workplaces and in our pocketbooks. Yet most of us are unaware of the enormity of the problem. Consider the following and then determine how concerned you are if others use drugs.

Drug Related Deaths

More deaths, diseases and disabilities are caused by substance abuse than any other preventable health condition. The substances being abused are not just drugs like cocaine, heroin and methamphetamine. Remember: alcohol and cigarettes are drugs too.

Of the more than **two million deaths** reported in the United States each year, **one in four is directly related to tobacco, alcohol or illicit drugs.**[1] Think about this: How large is the city or town you live in? Is it 5,000, 25,000, 300,000, 1 million people?

Every year tobacco kills nearly 440,000 people. Alcohol kills 100,000, and 16,000 people die as a result of illegal drugs. In other words, over **a half-million Americans die every year as a result of tobacco, alcohol and other illicit drugs.** Half a million people represents the populations of cities such as Oklahoma City, Washington D.C., and Portland, Oregon. And all those deaths are preventable!

INVOLVED: Parents' Connection to Drug Prevention

If we remove tobacco-related deaths from the equation, we still have almost 120,000 people dying each year as a result of alcohol and illegal drugs.[2] That's more than 300 people every day! If those numbers aren't a sobering thought and cause you great concern, then perhaps you still don't understand. This doesn't just mean 300 plus drug addicts or alcoholics die every day from the choices they made. It also represents the individuals who die as a result of someone else using alcohol or drugs.

While most of those deaths were indeed the result of an overdose, illness or accident resulting in the death of the user, many are merely innocent victims like the mom and dad and three children who were recently driving home from church on a Sunday morning. As they approached the red light they were talking about where to go for lunch. One of the kids suggested McDonald's. Another wanted to go to Chili's. The light turned green and the father proceeded into the intersection. No one saw the car approaching on their left. There was no way of knowing the driver had used drugs a few hours before and was still flying high as he plowed into their car. In the blink of an eye this family's life was changed forever. The father was pronounced dead on the scene, and the 12-year-old will probably be confined to a wheelchair the rest of his life – all because someone they never met chose to use drugs.

As a police officer, I've seen the twisted metal and smelled the burnt rubber. I've heard the moans of the injured and the silence of the dead. And whether it's the person on drugs who dies or an innocent child, parent or grandparent, the surviving family members are left to grieve the loss of their loved ones. They live the rest of their lives asking, "Why did this happen to our family? If only we had gone a different route that day. Or why didn't we leave two minutes earlier or two minutes later? Then this would have never happened."

Not long ago, I (Todd) met two wonderful parents, Nick and Cecile. Nick had agreed to talk to a group of high school students for an alcohol-awareness program. Ten years prior, a drunk driver killed his 19-year old daughter, Deena. I sat in the living room of the house where Deena spent the last years of her life. As we began to talk about the day of the crash, Cecile had to leave the room. She was overwhelmed by the grief of her loss despite the many years that had

Why Should You Care About Drug Abuse?

passed since Deena's death. Time does not heal the wound of losing a loved one.

As part of the program, Nick expressed a desire to show a video montage of family pictures. He wanted everyone to know the life that defined his daughter, not just the death that defined a tragedy. I spent several hours looking through all of the family photos as I put the video together. Every one of those pictures showed a wonderful and loving family with so many special moments. Nick requested I arrange the pictures to the song, *How am I Supposed to Live Without You,* performed by Michael Bolton. The chorus asks the question Nick and Cecile are still asking:

> *Tell me how am I supposed to live without you*
> *Now that I've been loving you so long?*
> *How am I supposed to live without you?*
> *How am I supposed to carry on*
> *When all that I've been living for is gone?*

After Deena's death many people tried to comfort Nick and Cecile by saying "at least you have so many good memories." Nick shared with me something that stung my heart. He said, "The memories were wonderful when they happened, but now that Deena is gone remembering them only brings us sorrow for what we lost."

Unfortunately, it often takes enduring the horrible ordeal of losing a child to an overdose or losing innocent family members in a car crash as a result of another's drug or alcohol use to understand the impact drugs have on our society. Yet over 300 families live out this nightmare every day in our country.

Have you ever visited the Vietnam Veteran's Memorial in Washington D.C.? I don't know one person who died in that war, but I was moved to tears when I stood before those granite panels and contemplated the 58,245 names of those who died during the sixteen years of conflict in Vietnam.

Imagine erecting a memorial twice the size of the Vietnam Veteran's Memorial ***each year*** with the 120,000 names of those who die as a result of alcohol and illegal drugs EVERY 365 days in America.

There will never be a memorial built for all of the victims of drugs and alcohol. However, I encourage you and your children to visit the Memorials on the *Partnership for a Drug-Free America* website. (www.drugfree.org/memorials). This website will touch your heart as you browse pictures and read stories of countless young people who have lost their lives as a result of drugs.

It is time we clearly understand the impact drugs and alcohol have on our society as a whole. It's important you understand your family is at risk. I don't say this to create a state of paranoia or panic but to create a state of awareness of how your family is affected and why you should care about alcohol and illegal drug use.

Do you care if others abuse alcohol or illegal drugs? Is it fair for you and your family to pay such a price?

Children are Paying a Price for Their Parent's Choices

Children are paying the price emotionally, physically and financially for their parents' alcohol and drug use. More than six million children under the age of 18 live with at least one parent who abuses alcohol or illicit drugs.[3]

(Todd) As a narcotics detective, I've gone into some pathetic home situations. I've been in the houses of drug addicts where children are living in squalor. I've seen roaches crawling on kids' toys, dirty diapers piled next to dishes on the kitchen counter and drug paraphernalia scattered on the coffee table. The stench was enough to make a person gag.

This doesn't just happen in inner-city neighborhoods. I've seen similar situations in middle- and upper-class homes as well. I remember an incident where my partners and I served a search warrant on a house with a methamphetamine lab. This lab was located in a middle-class neighborhood right across the street from the home of one of the police officers in my department.

As we walked up to the front door, we could smell the stench of chemicals coming from inside the house. When we entered the home, the mother and father were in the kitchen cooking methamphetamine, a process that uses highly explosive chemicals. The children were sleeping ten feet away.

The chemicals in the air were so strong we could feel them burning our eyes and throats. After we made the arrest and safely

Why Should You Care About Drug Abuse?

removed the children from the home, we had to use respirators to protect ourselves from the chemicals. As we searched the house, I'll never forget entering the parent's bedroom and seeing the children's hand-drawn pictures hanging on the walls. The pictures had big letters stating, "You're the best dad!" "You're the greatest mom in the world!" "#1 Parent!"

It was as if the parents were trying to assure themselves that what they were doing was okay, that none of this would affect their kids. These children had no way of knowing their parents had been sucked into an insidious addiction that resulted in endangering the entire family by producing methamphetamine in the middle of their kitchen.

The two innocent children were removed from the dangerous environment and placed in state supervision as their parents were taken to jail for manufacturing a dangerous drug. Unfortunately, these two children aren't alone. Each year more than 800,000 children are placed in the foster care system nationwide.[4] Seventy-five percent of those children are there because of drug and alcohol abuse. The detrimental impact on these children's emotional well-being and the likely damage to their future cannot be calculated.

Of course, it's your tax dollars paying the expenses for the parents' time in jail and the kids' foster care. Children found in methamphetamine labs often test positive for the drug as a result of accidental ingestion or exposure. No one knows what long-term health problems this family might encounter from breathing the toxic fumes day after day. But, not to worry, your tax dollars will likely be used to cover their medical bills as well.

Your tax dollars may also be needed to clean up the toxic contamination inside the house. The clean-up can run into the tens of thousands of dollars as the carpet and tile floors are replaced along with the sheetrock on the walls and ceilings. The chemicals are that toxic.

Of course, your tax dollars also cover the routine physical examinations narcotic officers undergo each year to make sure our livers, lungs and respiratory systems have not been affected by the drugs and chemicals we come into contact with day after day.

Do you care if others use drugs? Is it fair for innocent children to have to pay such a price? Is it fair *you* have to pay such a price?

Drug Use Increases Crime

Drug use creates crime for a variety of reasons. Drug use is an expensive habit. Therefore, it isn't unusual for those using drugs to turn to crime to support their habit. Many users commit crimes while under the influence of drugs. Every year the number of people arrested for crimes related to DUI, liquor-law violations, drunkenness, disorderly conduct and vagrancy runs into the millions of dollars. About half of state and federal prisoners who were convicted of violent crimes had been drinking or taking drugs at the time of their arrest.[5] All of these arrests require significant law enforcement resources.

For nearly a year, I was assigned to patrol a small rural community about forty-five minutes south of Las Vegas. One early morning I was sent to a house where someone had slashed the tires on the homeowner's car. As I took the police report, I received a call from the dispatcher about another car with slashed tires. Before I could even finish the first report three more victims called in reporting slashed tires. More than ten tires had been slashed involving multiple victims. Each victim required a separate police report. I spent most of the day driving from house to house taking those reports. Of course, it was the taxpayers who were paying my salary to take all those reports.

Later that day I caught the two high school boys responsible for the damage. The boys told me they slashed the tires because it made them laugh. Their laughter puzzled me, so I asked them why it was so funny to slash so many tires. They told me they were high on marijuana, and it made them laugh every time they cut a tire.

But why should you care about slashed tires by some kids high on drugs? They weren't your tires, and no one was hurt! And after all, insurance covered all the damage.

Well, the next time you complain about your insurance premiums going up, ask yourself again if you care about those tires being slashed. Every time someone on drugs does something stupid like breaking windows or running into a parked car, an insurance claim is filed. In return, insurance companies have no choice but to increase your rates.

Do you care if others use drugs? Is it fair you have to pay such a price?

Substance Abuse Costs Schools

Substance abuse and addiction adds at least $41 billion to the annual cost of elementary and secondary education. The costs are due to special education and tutoring needs, class disruption and violence, truancy, student assistance programs, children repeating grade levels, property damage, teacher turnover, injury and counseling.[6]

Schools across the country are cutting programs for lack of money. Maybe your son or daughter can't play their favorite sport because the money has to make up for that $41-billion loss. And although your own child isn't part of the problem, your tax dollars are going to pay for the added expenses your schools and community encounter.

Do you care if others use drugs? Is it fair you have to pay such a price?

Drugs in the Work Place

If you work outside your home, there's a good chance drugs are affecting your workplace. Consider these facts:

- 78 percent of the 11.8 million current adult illicit drug users are employed.[7]

- Alcohol and drug abuse costs American businesses $81 billion a year in lost productivity. $37 billion is due to premature death, and $44 billion is due to illness.[8]

- More than 60 percent of adults know someone who has reported for work under the influence of alcohol and other drugs.[9]

People who abuse drugs or those who have a family member who abuses drugs do not leave their problems at home. Their problems often overflow into the workplace resulting in absences, accidents and errors. Co-workers may feel added pressure to work harder, redo work or cover for the person with the drinking problems.

INVOLVED: Parents' Connection to Drug Prevention

Consider the mother who is putting her son's wet jeans into the dryer just before she goes to bed on Sunday night. In the bottom of the washer she finds a little bag with a green leafy substance. Her heart skips a beat. Surely this isn't what she thinks it is.

It's almost midnight. Should she wake her son up and confront him? Maybe she should take tomorrow off and spend the day with him. Then she remembers the big presentation due first thing in the morning. The entire office is depending on her. There's no way she has the luxury of staying home and working through this problem. It will have to wait until tomorrow night after she gets home from work.

The next day she tries to stay focused, but questions plague her thoughts. *How long has he been using drugs? Is he in the experimentation stage, or is he already addicted? How did I miss the warning signs?*

In the weeks to come, this once-loyal employee will be continually distracted as she is forced to take time off from work to meet with the principal at the school and transport her son to and from professional counseling sessions. Her job is important, but her son is more important. There is no choice. Her productivity begins to slip, and the entire office suffers from her son's bad decisions regarding drugs.

But it isn't just the children of the employees who affect the workplace. When employees use drugs, there can be serious consequences. Think about the construction worker who comes to work impaired. To those around him, he appears okay. His speech isn't slurred, and he looks fine; but because of his drug use he's just a little forgetful. On this particular day, he doesn't secure his safety harness appropriately and falls to his death, leaving behind a wife and two small children.

Or maybe it's the forklift operator who had a couple of beers at lunch. Thirty minutes later he jumps in the forklift, recklessly careens around a corner and kills a co-worker. Alcohol consumption and alcoholism are linked to as many as 40 percent of industrial fatalities and 47 percent of industrial injuries.[10]

Incidents like these have a tremendous impact on the productivity of a company, not to mention the company's profits. As a result, insurance premiums have soared; and employee benefits have been cut. This is certainly frustrating, especially if you and your family

50

Why Should You Care About Drug Abuse?

don't use drugs. But someone has to pay the price when others choose to use drugs.

Do you care if others use drugs? Is it fair you have to pay such a price?

Drug Abuse and Theft

As consumers, we're all affected by shoplifting and employee theft. One survey puts the annual loss for retail theft at around $43 billion.[11]

The regional security director of a large national retail store told me about three employees who had been accepting fraudulent checks from two customers in exchange for drugs. In a two-week time period, that retail chain took in $20,000 worth of bad checks as a result of those three employees. The suspects who wrote the bad checks were never arrested, and none of the money was recovered.

The security director said when the company took into consideration the amount of time it took to conduct the investigation, the loss of the $20,000, the firing of those 3 employees and hiring and training their replacements – it probably cost the company as much as $50,000. One incident, three employees – $50,000!

Roger Smith, the former Chairman of General Motors, has been quoted as stating that drug abuse costs General Motors $1 billion a year.[12] That cost is then passed on to the employees in loss of benefits and to the consumer in higher prices. Once again, this may not seem fair, but someone has to pay when others use drugs.

Do you care if others use drugs? Is it fair you have to pay such a price?

Drugs and the Health Care System

Here's another way we are affected by illegal drug use that most people never consider. An emergency room nurse once told me, "If it weren't for drugs and alcohol, I wouldn't have a job." In America there are about 1.5 million emergency room visits a year related to drug misuse or abuse.[13] This is a sobering thought considering we're already facing a crisis in many cities resulting from a shortage of critical care beds, as well as medical professionals, in our hospitals. Because of this shortage, ambulances are constantly being diverted to other hospitals to allocate the available beds and medical staff. This shortage could have a tremendous impact on your family some day.

Let's say your parents are in town visiting and your father suffers a heart attack on Friday morning. An ambulance arrives at your house, and time is critical to his survival. You know there's a great medical staff at the hospital only six blocks from your house. But as your father is being loaded into the ambulance, you're told no emergency room beds are available at that hospital. Several patients are taking up critical bed space because they overdosed on drugs the night before. It then takes the ambulance an additional 25 minutes to get across town through rush-hour traffic to another hospital with available bed space and staff to care for your father. Those 25 minutes can mean the difference in life and death.

That's exactly what happened during one Memorial Day weekend in Las Vegas. Eight patients suffering from drug overdoses while at a party went to the same hospital over a 12-hour period. Four of these patients received medical attention and were released within several hours. The other four had to be placed on ventilators in the critical-care unit. This one incident required nearly a quarter of the hospital beds in the emergency room due to the reckless behavior of drug users.

Remember, there are about 1.5 million drug-related episodes in emergency rooms every year. That's over 1,600 beds being used every day because someone chose to use drugs. And one of these days, they may be taking a bed you or one of your family members might desperately need.

The cost of health care climbs every year and millions of Americans are without it. And yet substance abuse is responsible for nearly $1 of every $4 spent by Medicare for inpatient hospital care and almost 20 percent of all Medicaid hospital costs.[14] Those are your tax dollars going to support Medicare and Medicaid!

Do you care if others use drugs? Is it fair you have to pay such a price?

The Parent Connection

Ideas to Help You Protect Your Child From Drugs

Who's going to Pay?

Hopefully, after reading this chapter, your blood pressure has gone up a few notches. That was the point! You need to feel angry about the price you and your family pay for others who use illegal drugs. And every time you walk in a store and see the inflated prices, or next year when your insurance rates go up again, or when April 15th rolls around and you write your check for your taxes, you will remember someone has to pay for those who are using drugs.

Now, take a few deep breaths and relax, but hold on to a bit of your frustration. Because one of the best things you can do to help your child avoid drugs is to passionately care about the misuse of drugs. You see, if you care deeply about this, your concern will rub off on your children, and they will also care.

The reverse is also true. The worst thing you can do is NOT care. If you don't care, your child may think you have no strong feelings one way or the other about drugs use. So when someone offers your child some marijuana, ecstasy or meth she may see nothing wrong with giving it a try. In fact, almost six times as many kids who think their parents *don't have strong feelings* about marijuana used the drug in the past month compared to teens who thought their parents would *strongly disapprove of its use*.[15]

This brings us to the third tip on the Parent Connection to Drug Prevention.

Tip #3 on DRUG PREVENTION

Teach Your Child to Care about the Misuse of Drugs.

INVOLVED: Parents' Connection to Drug Prevention

TRY THIS TIP!

Find a time when you and your children can spend 20 to 30 minutes of uninterrupted time together. This can be done over dinner, sitting around the family room or on a road trip. Begin by reading the following short story to your children.

Someone's Got to Pay

A mother called a family meeting where she announced, "Someone egged our neighbor's house last night, so I told Mr. Jones I would have all three of you paint his house this weekend."

"But we didn't do it!" the three children exclaimed in unison.

"Oh, I know you didn't," the mother replied. "I saw the little boy across the street doing it. But he would never offer to clean the mess up, so I told Mr. Jones the three of you would be happy to repaint his house this weekend."

"But that's not fair! Why do we have to do it?"

"Because someone has to do it," the mother explained.

"Oh, and by the way," the mother continued, "the little boy also spray-painted graffiti on another neighbor's car. I told that neighbor I would deduct half of your allowances for the next three years to pay for the damage."

"Why?" the three cried in protest. "We didn't do it!"

"Because," the mother replied, "the little boy across the street doesn't have any money, and someone has to pay for his wrongdoings."

"And one last thing," the mother said, "the little boy across the street played in our backyard this afternoon while you were in school, and he forgot to close the gate. I'm sorry kids, but your dog got out of the yard and was run over by a car and was killed."

And the three children cried.

After reading the story:

1. Ask your children to share their feelings about what they just heard. How would they feel if you asked them to do what the mother in the story asked her children to do?

2. After you finish discussing the story, read this entire chapter together as a family. At the conclusion of each section, let your children respond when the question is asked, "Is it fair you have to pay such a price?"

3. Once you've finished reading the chapter, read the short story one more time and ask your children to find the similarities between the story and what happens when people use drugs.

4. Then conclude the discussion by explaining to your children that this is exactly why you do not want them to have anything to do with drugs. Explain that while they might not be able to change the hearts and minds of people using drugs, they can choose to be responsible for themselves.

References

[1] The John Hopkins University, *Facts About Substance Abuse: The Human Cost of Substance Abuse,* Baltimore, Md. 2004.

[2] United States Department of Health and Human Services, *Substance Abuse - A National Challenge: Prevention, Treatment and Research at HHS,* 2006.

[3] National Household Survey on Drug Abuse, The NHSDA Report, *Children Living with Substance- Abusing or Substance-Dependent Parents,* 2003.

[4] U.S. Department of Health and Human Services, *Trends in Foster Care and Adoption FY 2000-FY 2005,* 2007.

[5] Schneider Institute for Health Policy, (Brandeis University for The Robert Wood Johnson Foundation.) *Substance Abuse: The Nation's Number One Health Problem. Key Indicators for Policy Update,* February 2001.

[6] The National Center on Addiction and Substance Abuse (CASA), *Malignant Neglect: Substance Abuse and America's Schools,* 2001.

[7] U.S. Department of Health and Human Services, Press Release – *HHS Report Shows Drug Use Rates Stable, Youth Tobacco Use Declines,* 2001.

[8] US Department of Health and Human Services Substance Abuse and Mental Health Services Administration, *Substance Abuse and Mental Health Statistics Sourcebook,* Rockville, MD, 1995. As Reported in *U.S. Department of Labor in the 21st Century,* 2007.

[9] Hazeldon Foundation, "The Impact of Addiction in the Workplace," *Occupational Medicine,* 4(2)2007.

[10] M. Bernstein, and J. Mahoney, *Management Perspectives on Alcoholism: The Employer's Stake in Alcoholism Treatment.*

[11] University of Florida, *National Retail Security Survey Final Report,* 2002.

[12] Health and Safety Services, Inc. *What Every Employer Should Know about Drug-Abuse in the Workplace,* 2004.

[13] Drug Abuse Warning Network (DAWN), Office of Applied Studies, *Drug Abuse Warning Network, 2005: National Estimates of Drug-Related Emergency Department Visits,* 2007.

[14] The Schneider Institute for Health Policy and The Robert Wood Johnson Foundation, *Substance Abuse: The Nation's Number One Health Problem,* 2001.

[15] The National Center on Addiction and Substance Abuse at Columbia University, *Non-Medical Marijuana II: Rite of Passage or Russian Roulette?* April 2004.

Chapter 4

What Every Parent Needs To Know About Drugs

While the information on drug and alcohol abuse among our children can be disturbing, there is good news. As previously, stated the overall drug use among American teenagers is presently on a downward trend. The following chart shows the findings from a survey taken by the National Institute on Drug Abuse.

Drug Use Among American Teens[1]

The numbers indicate the percentage of students who have tried the drug at least once.

Drug	8th Grade			10th Grade			12th Grade		
	1993	2000	2007	1993	2000	2007	1993	2000	2007
Heroin	1.4	1.9	1.3	1.3	2.2	1.5	1.1	2.4	1.5
Crack Cocaine	1.7	3.1	2.1	1.8	3.7	2.3	2.6	3.9	3.2
Meth	N/A	4.2	1.8	N/A	6.9	2.8	N/A	7.9	3.0
Ecstasy	N/A	4.3	2.3	N/A	7.3	5.2	N/A	11.0	6.5
Cocaine	2.9	4.5	3.1	3.6	6.9	5.3	6.1	8.6	7.8
Amphetamines	11.8	9.9	6.5	14.9	15.7	11.1	15.1	15.6	11.4
Inhalants	19.4	17.9	15.6	17.5	16.6	13.6	17.4	14.2	10.5
Marijuana	12.6	20.3	14.2	24.4	40.3	31.0	35.3	48.8	41.8
Cigarettes	45.3	40.5	22.1	56.3	55.1	34.6	61.9	62.5	46.2
Alcohol	55.7	51.7	38.9	71.6	71.4	61.7	80.0	80.3	72.2

INVOLVED: Parents' Connection to Drug Prevention

When Does Drug Experimentation Begin?

Many parents start worrying about their children experimenting with drugs about the time they start driving and dating. Unfortunately, those parents are already a few years behind the facts.

By the 8th grade:[2]
39 percent have consumed alcohol
22 percent have smoked cigarettes
14 percent have used marijuana
16 percent have used inhalants

By the 12th grade:

72 percent have consumed alcohol
46 percent have smoked cigarettes
42 percent have used marijuana
11 percent have used inhalants

The Magical Age of 14

While it is obvious drug use accelerates throughout the teenage years, it's also important to realize the difference a single year can make. Most amazing is the difference between a 13-year-old and a 14-year old. Whether it's the result of going from middle school to high school or 14-year-olds beginning to sprout their wings and venture further away from home, it's difficult to say. Whatever the cause, it appears the risk for drug use significantly increases at age 14.

Compared to 13-year-olds 14-year-old are:

- Two times more likely to be offered cocaine
- Three times more likely to be offered ecstasy
- Three times more likely to be offered marijuana
- Four times more likely to be offered prescription drugs[3]

> **The legal age to drink alcohol is 21.**
> **The average age for a first drink is 14.**[4]

The Girls Beat the Boys!

It's true! The girls are edging past the boys. But this is one race no one can cheer about. While overall drug use is going down among teens (both girls and guys), first-time users are more likely to be girls than boys. Girls have taken the lead in first-time use in cigarettes, alcohol, marijuana and prescription drugs.[5] And this trend is starting as young as 8th grade. In the past, boys have always led the way in drug use, and at times it was a significant lead – until now.

It's imperative we get the message to our girls. This is one race they do not want to win! It's the girls – not boys – who are more vulnerable to the risks of drugs. Not only do girls tend to get drunk faster than guys, they also tend to develop an addiction to drugs easier than their male counterparts. Girls also run a far greater risk than guys of dealing with depression when using drugs.

These issues will be discussed in more detail later in the book.

How Does It Begin?

It's Monday morning. Word has spread quickly through Mrs. Johnson's fifth grade class that Connor and Caleb got high last night from sniffing airplane glue. Some are saying Connor actually passed out. Students whisper and giggle as they strain to sneak a peek at the two infamous characters. Everyone wants to see if they look or act different now that they've taken the plunge.

Although it wasn't your son who did the sniffing, all the talk has left him wondering, "What was it like? How did it make them feel?" Then he remembers the glue in the cabinet in your utility room and wonders if it would provide the same high as Connor and Caleb experienced.

Two blocks down the street the bell rings at the middle school, and students rush through the halls to get to first-period class. Before the next bell rings, news that Brent and Amber got drunk last night has already circulated throughout most of the eighth grade. By noon, the information filters all the way down to the sixth graders. Although it wasn't your daughter who consumed the alcohol, she is left wondering, "What was it like? How did it taste? How did it make them feel?"

INVOLVED: Parents' Connection to Drug Prevention

Her thoughts then shift to the beer in her best friend's refrigerator, and she wonders if anyone would notice if they snuck a few cans out for their next Friday-night sleepover.

- **39 percent of 8th graders have tried alcohol**
- **18 percent have been drunk[6]**

Who are Today's Drug Dealers?

If kids want to get high, all they have to do is look under the kitchen sink, in the family desk drawer, in mom's bathroom cabinet or in the garage for a wide range of legal products to produce the necessary fumes to get high. Spray paint, nail polish remover, felt tip markers or glue will do the trick.

Finding drugs like marijuana and ecstasy are usually easy to locate at school. I *(Todd)* remember when I was a kid I was always told to stay away from the stranger on the corner who might try to give me a sugar cube or stamps. The idea was that some scary old man was going to try to lure me and all my friends into getting addicted to LSD by eating sugar cubes or licking stamps that had been tampered with. That was the image of a drug dealer in the '70's.

If you happen to be one of those parents who drop your child off at school and nervously look around for the vicious old man hanging around the play ground handing out drugs to unsuspecting kids, you're wasting your time! He isn't there. I'm not sure he was there even when I was a kid.

Don't get me wrong. Drug dealers certainly exist in our local schools, but they typically aren't scary old men. The drug dealers of today are your child's classmates and the older siblings of your child's classmates.

Let me explain. Let's say your 7th grade son tells you he's going across the street to see his best friend, Josh. Now Josh has a big brother, Jake, who is a sophomore in high school. When Josh and your son go down in Josh's basement to shoot some pool, they find Jake smoking some pot.

Jake then asks the two 7th graders if they want to try some. He gives them a few puffs. He doesn't want them to get too high because he doesn't want their parents suspecting what's going on. Jake probably thinks he is doing Josh and your son a favor. He sees it as his responsibility to show the boys the right way to smoke a joint. After all, it's much safer to learn from someone you know than from a stranger, right? Jake then explains that if they want more pot in the future there will be a small fee since this stuff doesn't come free.

So, as you see, the dealer isn't some unscrupulous stranger looking for another child victim to be his next moneymaker. While that might possibly happen, most kids are introduced to drugs by a friend or relative. Occasionally it's actually the parents providing their children with drugs and alcohol. Then when their children's friends come over, those kids are welcome to join in the family fun.

Maybe you saw the tragic story on television about the beautiful young high school girl who died while spending the night at a friend's house. The girls had used some drugs at a sleepover, and something went horribly wrong. When the girl became ill, no one in the house – not even the parents – called for medical help. The girl's father didn't even know she had gotten sick until the call came the next morning that his daughter was dead.

If you don't know the parents of your child's friends beyond that wave from the door as you drop them off, get to know them better. Not all adults share your values and belief system. Remember, you are entrusting your child's life to those people.

How Difficult is It to Find Drugs?

It's probably easier for the average 15- or 16-year-old to find marijuana than it is for an adult because most schools have something like a living network existing among the students. I *(Todd)* asked a group of high school students if they thought they would have any trouble finding marijuana. They all agreed that after asking four to five people they could find what they wanted. According to a national study, 37 percent of 8th graders, 69 percent of 10th graders and 84 percent of seniors stated marijuana is accessible to those who want it.[7]

INVOLVED: Parents' Connection to Drug Prevention

I looked very young when I was a rookie cop, and I was chosen to hang out at a local high school during lunchtime to see if I could locate some marijuana. The goal was not to target the high school students, but to find adults who were supplying them. I met a few students at a fast food restaurant, and it wasn't long before their conversation turned to getting high. I asked about finding some marijuana and one of the students told me he was out of his supply. I asked another student; and he gave me the phone number to his connection, a 19-year-old who graduated the year before. I placed a call to the dealer, and within a few hours I arranged to buy marijuana from someone I never met. Schools are like a huge Internet search engine. One kid asks another for marijuana; and poof, he gets multiple hits.

Let me explain Drug Economics 101. Let's say I'm a 20-year-old college student, and I know a drug dealer who grows his own pot. I go over to his house one afternoon, and I buy an ounce of bud for $100. (Bud is slang for marijuana. It refers to the flower or bud on the marijuana plant.)

Now I have no intentions of smoking the entire ounce. I have a far better plan that will benefit both my drug habit and my pocketbook. I divide the $100 worth of marijuana into four quarter ounces. I keep a quarter ounce for my own personal use, and then I go over to Jack's house. Jack is a senior in high school. I sell him a quarter ounce for $35. Then I go a few blocks to Ashley's house, and she and her cousin Drew both buy a quarter ounce for $35 each. Now I'd say that's a pretty good deal. I just got a quarter ounce of marijuana, and it didn't cost me anything. In fact, I have a little change left in my pocket. Not bad for an hour's worth of work!

Ashley and Drew are also pleased with the transaction, because by the time I left their house, they were already rolling their stash into individual cigarettes. Then they turn around and sell the cigarettes for a few bucks each to kids at school.

As you can see, most drug dealers begin as casual users who realize there is money to be made that will pay for their own habit and provide them with some extra spending money. Who says today's teens don't understand economics and the marketplace!

While I was working undercover I met Tony at a party and learned he was selling ecstasy. I bought a few pills from him, and he told me he could sell me whatever I wanted. I called him a few days later and made an arrangement to purchase 1,000 ecstasy pills. I arrested Tony when he showed up with the pills. Later I learned he was a college student at the local university. Tony came from an upper-middle-class family, and his parents bought him a condo and were paying for his college. He told me he started using ecstasy at parties and learned if he bought larger quantities of pills at the same time, the price per pill dropped. Tony and his roommate made a business plan and a cash-flow chart in which they detailed out their costs and profits. Not only did they realize they could make money selling ecstasy, but they also started selling LSD, marijuana and methamphetamine. Tony furnished his entire condo with his drug proceeds. He and his roommate even mapped out their exit strategy once they had finished buying everything on their shopping list. Unfortunately for them, they met me first. They were lucky I wasn't a rival drug dealer willing to do whatever it took to eliminate the competition.

Imagine the shock and grief when there is a knock on the door to inform a parent that their child is dead because of a drug transaction gone bad. Such was the case for Mike, a retired 21-year veteran of a federal law enforcement agency. Mike's son had been attending college; and despite his dad's wishes for him to live at home, he moved into his own condo. Mike had no idea his son started using drugs and certainly never expected he was selling them until there was a knock at his door. That was when local police informed Mike his son was found in his car, shot four times outside his condo, killed by a rival drug dealer.

The Parent Connection

Ideas to Help You Protect Your Child From Drugs

When and What to Say about Drugs

When to Start Talking About Drugs

Parents need to talk to their children about the dangers of drugs before they begin hearing about this from their friends. That means before they enter school and experience peer pressure. The earlier you begin to share your values regarding drugs the more likely this concept will become ingrained in their brains.

Before I *(Marilyn)* started school, I remember learning the phrase, "Step on a crack, and you'll break your mother's back." To this very day I find myself adjusting my steps to avoid stepping on cracks. How absurd! Especially considering my mother died over 20 years ago! As I'm walking down the street, I tell myself, "Go ahead – step on the crack. She's not going to care!" And then two minutes later I realize I'm adjusting my steps again. It's amazing how the things we learn when we're really young stay with us for a lifetime! This can work in your favor when you're instilling values.

The following are a few reasons why it is best to begin educating your children at an early age.

Reason #1: Your child needs to know *your family does not do drugs* BEFORE someone offers him that first sniff of glue, taste of beer or puff on a cigarette.

Reason #2: Most seven-year-olds still believe everything their parents tell them; but once they reach double digits, they begin to question everything their parents say.

Reason #3: Most eight-year-olds still think their parents are cool and want to please them. But the day is rapidly approaching when Mom and Dad will no longer be cool and the child will be focused on pleasing his or her peers.

Tip #4 on DRUG PREVENTION

Start talking about the dangers of drugs when your child is young and never stop.

HERE ARE SOME IDEAS TO CONSIDER!

Protecting Children from Drugs

Young people who find themselves bored and unsupervised are more likely to use drugs. Therefore, consider the following ideas:

- **Make sure your child is well supervised after school.** It's those first few hours after school (between 3:00 and 6:00) when most young people make their drug deals. And young people who are not regularly monitored by their parents are four times more likely to use drugs.[8] If you aren't available to be home after school, then make sure your child is involved in after-school activities. This can include sports, music, art lessons, scouts, church and/or community activities. And don't take the attitude, "But my kid's a good kid. He wouldn't do drugs." It's not about being good or bad. It's about being lonely and bored. Teens who say they are "often bored" are 50 percent more likely to smoke, drink, get drunk and use illegal drugs than teens who aren't bored and lonely.[9]

- **Don't allow your child to have friends in your home when you aren't there**; and don't allow your child to be in a friend's home where there is no parental supervision. Whether it's a couple of curious seven-year-olds or a 17-

INVOLVED: Parents' Connection to Drug Prevention

year-old guy and his girlfriend hanging out together for a couple of hours before Mom and Dad get home from work, neither scenario has the makings of a healthy situation and should be avoided at all costs.

- **Know where your child is at all times**. This isn't so difficult when your child is early elementary school age, but once he has wheels and can leave home – on a bicycle or in a car – keeping track of Junior becomes much more difficult. And asking typical parental-type questions – "Where are you going? Who will be with you? What time will you be home?" – may cause your child to resent your intrusion into his world. But you can reduce his frustration by setting the example. Make it a point to always volunteer where you are going and when you will be home. If your plans change or if you're going to be late, call your child and inform him. By setting the example for him, your list of questions won't be so intrusive; they will merely be a way of returning the same common courtesy you have demonstrated to him throughout the years.

- **Beware of the lazy days of summer** when kids have nothing to do. This is when so many kids experiment with drugs for the very first time. Each day in June and July over 6,300 youth try their first joint of marijuana. That's 40 percent more per day than during the rest of the year.[10]

- **Take note of how much spending money** your child has available. Drugs cost money; and kids who have access to $25 or more a week in spending money are nearly twice as likely as those with less money to smoke, drink and use illegal drugs; and they're more than twice as likely to get drunk.[11]

- **Take note of your child's stress level**. Teens can find themselves weighed down with stress from a wide array of reasons – academics, sports, social issues, etc. And many teens are desperate to find relief. In fact, teens dealing with high stress are twice as likely as low-stress teens to smoke, drink, get drunk and use illegal drugs.[12]

Continued Education

A compliant eight-year-old girl may say no to drugs simply because that's what her mother told her to say. But that's not going to be enough to stop her when she's 16 and in the arms of an 18-year-old boy who's promising her if she swallows a little pill she'll have the experience of a lifetime. So drug education must start early and continue throughout life. And while you're teaching your children to say no to drugs, don't forget to explain why drugs are dangerous. The old adage, "Because I said so," isn't enough for older children, especially in today's society.

Warning for Your Child

Your drug education and instruction needs to be focused on the fact that your child is the most precious thing in your life, and you will do anything it takes to protect her from the destructive power of drugs. Therefore, she needs to know if you observe changes in her behavior that are characteristic of drug use, you will waste no time in confronting her with your concerns and seeking outside help from a professional who is trained to deal with issues related to drug use

References

[1] National Institute on Drug Abuse. *Monitoring the Future,* April 2008.
[2] Ibid.
[3] The National Center on Addiction and Substance Abuse (CASA) at Columbia University, *Teen Survey Reveals: Teen Parties Awash in Alcohol, Marijuana and Illegal Drugs – Even when Parent are Present.* 2006.
[4] National Institutes of Health (NIH) – National Institute on Alcohol Abuse and Alcoholism (NIAAA), *Alcohol Alert: Underage Drinking.* January 2006.
[5] Office of National Drug Control Policy: Executive Office of the President, *A New Analysis: Recent Trends, Risk Factors and Consequences – Girls and Drugs,* 2006.
[6] National Institute on Drug Abuse, *Monitoring the Future,* April 2008.
[7] Ibid.
[8] Metzler, Rusby, and Biglan, Oregon Research Institute, *Community Builders and Success: Monitoring After-School Activities,* 1999.
[9] The National Center on Addiction and Substance Abuse (CASA), *Teen Survey: High Stress, Frequent Boredom, Too Much Spending Money: Triple Threat that Hikes Risk of Teen Substance Abuse,* 2003.
[10] Substance Abuse and Mental Health Services Administration (SAMHSA) *Seasonality of Youth's First-Time Use of Marijuana, Cigarettes, or Alcohol,* June 4, 2004.
[11] The National Center on Addiction and Substance Abuse (CASA), *Teen Survey, 2003.*
[12] Ibid.

Chapter 5

What's Wrong with a Little Experimenting?

No doubt you've heard people say, "What's it going to hurt if a kid gets a little dizzy from a few sniffs of glue or feels a slight buzz after drinking a beer or even gets a little high from smoking a joint of marijuana? After all, kids are going to be kids."

That's a good question. And the truth is few kids suffer severe consequences the first time they get drunk or use drugs. But what if your child's first experience with drugs was a good one? There's a good chance he will try it again and then maybe again and again.

It's sort of like the old Lay's Potato Chip commercial that used to be on television, "I bet you can't eat just one." Now if you happen to be like millions of Americans who love the crisp, salty taste of potato chips, then you know the commercial is right. It's impossible for many of us to stop with just one chip. After the first experience you're hooked, and you want more and more chips. In fact, just the mere mention of potato chips may be sending some of you to the pantry right now. But there's a big difference in potato chips and illicit drugs.

While a sniff of glue or a can of beer or a joint of marijuana may seem harmless to some adults, if the first experience caused that kid to float two or three inches off the ground then that might just be enough for him to want to do it again. But next time he'll probably be striving to float 6 inches off the ground – or maybe a foot. And now he longs for his next opportunity when he can sniff, drink or smoke and experience an even greater high.

INVOLVED: Parents' Connection to Drug Prevention

Understanding Addiction

Everyone enjoys feeling good! And one of the reasons we as humans are able to feel good is because our brains produce chemicals that send out positive messages when we do something enjoyable. For example, you might get a surge of the "feel-good" chemical when you eat ice cream, or maybe it's shopping or a kiss that produces these chemicals in your brain. So anytime you feel pleasure you can know chemicals in your brain are sending positive messages encouraging you to repeat the activity.

Now there's no denying drugs can also make a person feel good. The reason the buzz or high occurs is because drugs such as tobacco, alcohol, marijuana, ecstasy, cocaine, methamphetamine and heroin can hack into a person's brain and mimic the feel-good chemicals. So as soon as the person is feeling high, he knows the drug has successfully hacked into his brain and the feel-good chemical is being released.

Once the brain catches on to what's happening, it cuts back its own feel-good chemical and the exuberant high is replaced with a depressing low. This may also include muscle aches and pain, even anxiety attacks. These are called **withdrawal symptoms.** They leave the user hating how he feels, and he's now consumed with the thought of using drugs again so he'll feel better.

Each time he uses, the drugs hack into his brain and cause another massive flood of feel-good chemicals. And each time he uses he feels good again – for a little while. But before long the chemicals in his brain are so messed up the highs are less high, and the lows get lower and lower. Desperate to just feel normal, he begins using more drugs, stronger drugs or a combination of drugs. This is a phenomenon known as **tolerance.**

Pretty soon the user has difficulty feeling any pleasure at all. Not even ice cream, shopping or a kiss brings pleasure. He is now sinking deeper into depression. And whether he realizes it or not, he has no stopping mechanism. The drugs have so messed up his brain he literally cannot stop using the very substance that is destroying his life. His entire life is consumed with the need to use more drugs as the disease of **addiction** has now successfully infected his brain.

> **Addiction is a disease of the brain.**

(Marilyn) My father recently passed away from Alzheimer's, also a disease of the brain. What a horrible experience to have 85 years of memories fade away into darkness while you lose control of all bodily functions. But the big difference in the disease my father experienced and the disease of a drug addict is that the drug addict had a choice. On a given date in time the drug addict chose to take that very first drug. Had he simply said no to drugs, he never would have suffered from the disease of addiction.

This does not mean there is no hope for those addicted to drugs. There is. But a recovering drug addict has an unbelievably difficult challenge ahead. The changes that have occurred in his brain because of the drugs will be the very thing that will make it difficult to control the all-consuming cravings and to have the necessary determination to stop using.

In fact, it's next to impossible for compulsive drug users to stop on their own. In most cases it will require a tremendous amount of support and assistance from family members as well as professional help from experts regarding available treatment, rehab and detox centers. Even at that, there is NO quick, magical cure for drug abusers. Addiction is considered a **chronic disease,** which means **relapse** is possible at any time. Therefore, a successful treatment for addiction is where the person learns to manage his illness and increase the time between relapses until hopefully the day comes when there are no more relapses.

Other Concerns

Beyond the concerns of addiction, drugs also cause potential health problems including memory loss, problems in learning, mood swings, depression and poor judgment. These health problems can lead to automobile accidents, sexual activity and violence. But let's not forget the greatest concern of all – death as a result of an overdose or suicide.

INVOLVED: Parents' Connection to Drug Prevention

"Oh, but I'll be careful and stop before I overdose," says the cocky high school football player as he snorts a line of cocaine before the big game. But using drugs is like playing Russian Roulette. No one ever knows if the first time, the tenth time or maybe the twentieth time will be the last time for everything!

Today I received a call from a friend whose coworker's son died of an accidental drug overdose. He was only 16-years-old. How many more kids have to die? How many more parents have to be left asking why?

Where Does It Happen

As previously stated, the majority of drug transactions among teens take place between 3:00 and 6:00 in the afternoon before mom and dad get home from work. While some kids might go to their room, close the door and proceed to get stoned in the privacy of their own bedrooms, most kids prefer to make this a group activity. A couple of bored 8th graders might meet at their usual spot to get their afternoon high. Perhaps it's a backyard, an alley or a vacant lot.

It isn't unusual for a flier to circulate through a high school stating:

HOUSE PARTY
BRING YOUR BOOZE AND DRUGS
BRING THIS FLIER TO GET IN

From a teen's perspective, an individual's home is a great place for a party. The young people know they don't have to worry about being arrested for underage drinking or consuming drugs in a private residence. It's more difficult for undercover police to infiltrate the party, and in most cases the police can't enter a home without a search warrant.

More than likely the party referred to in the flier is taking place while the unsuspecting parents are out-of-town. But there's also the possibility it's taking place at a home where the parents are fully aware of what's happening. These parents are considered cool because they have no problem with kids using their home to party! In fact, these parents might even enjoy getting high right along with their young guests.

What's Wrong with a Little Experimenting?

Or perhaps the parents smoked a little pot or did a few lines of coke back in their college days. Today they might have a successful life with no repercussions from their carefree days of experimentation. So they've convinced themselves it's safer for kids to get drunk or high in a home where there is adult supervision than off by themselves. But there are a few problems with this concept. This mom and dad made a choice one day to stop before they did any real damage to themselves or to anyone else, but for some people the damage is done before they can choose to stop.

Consider Danielle Heard, a 21-year-old full of life. She experimented with ecstasy three times. The third time killed her. Or consider Leonard "Len" Bias who was drafted by the Boston Celtics. He was on top of the world, and many compared him to Michael Jordan. The guy was in top physical condition. He had everything going for him. He was supposed to be the savior of the Celtics, but he chose to do drugs, and at age 22 he died.

The point is no one ever knows how his body will react to drugs. One time the person may experience an amazing high, and the next time the drug could kill him.

The Dangers of Drugs

The problems associated with drug use are extensive. The following are some of the more common concerns. They will be discussed in more detail in the following chapters.

- Drugs can damage a person's:
    heart
    kidneys
    liver
    brain
- Drugs can lead to:
    Memory loss
    Loss of concentration
    Loss of balance and coordination
    Slow reflexes
    Decreased athletic ability

INVOLVED: Parents' Connection to Drug Prevention

    Personality changes
    Depression
    Mood swings
    Panic attacks
    Paranoia
    Rage and anger
    Loss of friends
    Drop in grades
    Sleeplessness
    Fatigue
    Blurred vision
    Loss in appetite
    Weight loss
    Anorexia
    Death

Warning Signs

Note: It isn't unusual for a young person to have some of the following symptoms without being on drugs. But if you see a sudden change in the behavior of your child with several of these symptoms, it's time to take action.

    Isolation - withdrawn from family and friends
    Loss of interest in sports or other hobbies
    Depression
    Change in type of friends
    Drop in school attendance and grades
    Fatigue
    Change in eating and sleeping habits
    Lack of interest in personal appearance
    Persistent red eyes, runny nose and cough
    Mood swings
    Paranoia
    Anxiety attacks, irritability or rage
    Lying to parents and friends
    Stealing

Drug Paraphernalia to Watch For

Small plastic sack with dried leaves
Rolling papers
Butane lighters
Pipes
Suckers
Pacifiers
Glow sticks
Rags soaked with chemicals – gasoline, paint, etc.
Paint on your child's clothes or face

Also Watch For

- Alcohol disappearing from the liquor cabinet or watered-down bottles in the liquor cabinet

- Disappearance of prescribed medications from the medicine cabinet

- Disappearance of household products and chemicals such as spray paint, gasoline, nail polish remover, whiteout, markers, prescription drugs or over-the-counter drugs

- Increased use of breath mints, chewing gum, perfume or cologne to cover odors

- Sudden use of incense, candles or deodorizers

The Parent Connection

Ideas to Help You Protect Your Child From Drugs

Stating Your Values

Today's television, movies, and music make it possible for our children to be exposed to the drug culture 24/7. The Internet opens the door for our children to be exposed to drug information and misinformation like never before. Go to any search engine and type in the word "marijuana," and you will find over *20 million* Internet sites on the subject. Some of the most prominent websites not only offer information and personal stories describing detailed experiences but also provides video clips that teach the novice how to use the drug. If you know where to look on the Internet (and many kids do) you can even find drugs for sale. While it may be very difficult to limit our children's exposure to the drug culture, you can create an anti-drug culture in your home by setting standards and educating your children to the dangers of drugs. So the next tip on the Parent Connection to Drug Prevention is:

> **Tip # 5 on DRUG PREVENTION**
> Teach Your Child Your Values on Drugs

No doubt your child has been raised to abide by rules. There are a number of rules in your child's life you may waiver on from time to time. Some rules will be bent or eventually done away with; curfews will be expanded and freedoms will be granted. But your child needs to know your stand on drugs will *never* change. After all, parents never hold their heads up high and proclaim to the world, "My child is addicted to drugs." And there is no age where drug addiction is a good thing.

Therefore, it is important you state emphatically where you stand on the use of drugs. You must make your stand clear, and you must state it over and over again.

HERE ARE SOME GREAT IDEAS!

Teaching Your Values

- Repeat the following statement to your child so often that it becomes ingrained in his brain:

    OUR FAMILY DOES NOT DO DRUGS

    Let your child also overhear you saying this phrase to your friends and relatives. Hearing this statement over and over, year after year, will make it easier for him to say, "No, thanks, I don't do drugs," when asked by a friend to sniff some glue or smoke some pot.

> My Family Does Not Do Drugs.
> I Do Not Do Drugs.

- A passing comment about drugs now and then is far better than long, boring lectures. And as often as possible, interject a positive comment or subtle praise. For example, let your child know drug use among American teens is going down. That's an important fact to share with your child considering most young people want to fit in with their peers. Perhaps over dinner you could casually say something like, "I read the other day that most high school students have never tried marijuana, cocaine or heroin. In fact, the overall use of drugs among American teens is dropping. I'm really impressed with your generation. You guys really seem to have your heads screwed on straight!"

- Look for opportunities to talk about drug use. When you're watching television with your child, talk about the people on the programs or commercials who are drinking, using drugs or smoking. Include in your conversation the expense of supporting such a habit, the impact on family members, as well as the health issues associated with using drugs.

    I *(Todd)* recently took my teenage son to a rock concert where some very rude, inconsiderate and law-breaking adults were smoking marijuana down the row from our seats. As much as I was disgusted with the situation, it afforded me an opportunity to ask my son if he had ever smelled marijuana before. He said he had only smelled that odor once but didn't know it was marijuana. Then he said, "That stuff stinks. I don't know why people are so stupid and smoke that stuff." He knew I was disgusted at the situation (expression of my values) and he was genuinely disgusted too (expression of his values!) Wow, it was great to hear him voice his own attitude about drug use!

- Role play with your child by asking, "What would you say if someone asked you if you wanted to try some drugs?" If he shrugs his shoulders and says, "I don't know." take this opportunity to teach him helpful tips on refusal skills.

    For example, explain to him, "When someone offers you a beer or a joint of marijuana, quickly reply with the simple words, 'No, thanks!' By doing this, you're demonstrating you are a secure, confident person. Yet, a person who timidly replies, 'Well.... I don't know if I should.' is demonstrating weakness. This type of response also encourages continued pressure."

    Inform your child that it's possible the simple words, "No, thanks," will be all that's needed. But help your child think through how to respond to those who are more persistent in their encouragement to try drugs. This can be done by using

What's Wrong with a Little Experimenting?

role reversal. Have your child give you a pressure line such as, "You want to smoke a joint?" Then you respond with the following responses:

> ➢ No, thanks. My parents know more about drugs than I do, and they will know if I start using.
> ➢ No, thanks. My parents told me if they ever thought I used drugs they would drug test me.
> ➢ No, thanks. My parents told me if someone gives me drugs, they will visit that kid's parents and call the police to report it.

Have fun with your child with continued, spontaneous role playing throughout the years. As your child is getting out of the car to go to school or heading upstairs to go to bed, call out to him in deep, gruff voice, "Hey, kid – you want some drugs?"

Continued role playing not only empowers your child to have a strong, ready answer, it also serves as a constant reminder that you are very serious about him saying NO to drugs.

- Encourage your older children to be positive role models by taking a strong stand against drugs. Help them understand their younger siblings are always watching them and looking up to them. Encourage your older children to enthusiastically join in family discussions and role-playing games as an example to the younger children in your household.

- When a tragic, drug-related accident occurs in your community, talk about the details over dinner or while driving your child to soccer practice. Discuss the pain the family members of the victims must be experiencing. Talk about the fact that this type of pain never goes away. And conclude the conversation by stating, "This is just one more reason I always want you to say, 'No, thanks!' when someone offers you drugs."

HERE'S ANOTHER IDEA!
The Pain of Addiction

A young lady recently sent me (Marilyn) the following letter describing the pain she and her family experienced because of drug addiction. Read the letter to your children and then discuss what it must be like to have a family member addicted to drugs.

*It's amazing my brother is still alive! He just turned 35. Ten years ago he was told **IF** he lived to be 35, it would be a miracle. You see, my brother is a drug addict. It started one night when he was a curious 13-year-old. He and some of his buddies decided to try drinking some beer. He never dreamed that evening would begin a life-long battle of addiction, but it did.*

I can't remember life before my brother got into drugs, but I have vivid memories of the pain my family has endured because of his choice to use drugs. Perhaps the worst part was the constant fear. My brother had become extremely volatile, and I never knew when he might explode in a fit of rage. I can remember many nights around the dinner table when light discussion would unpredictably erupt into a fiery fight between my dad and brother.

I spent many nights locked in a room of the house crying out of fear, not only for my own safety, but much more, a fear that my brother would kill my dad. I would wake up in the night shaking if Mom and Dad's voices got loud, thinking something bad must be going on; or if I heard a chair being pushed in under the table down in the kitchen because it triggered the emotions aroused when my brother would jump up during dinner to yell at Dad.

Over the next five to ten years, my fear changed from a fear of what my brother might do to one of us to what he might do to himself. As time had gone on, he had made many attempts to overcome his addiction. He got help from many different sources, but nothing worked. He lived many years in deep

What's Wrong with a Little Experimenting?

depression, and the only thing that seemed to give temporary relief was more drugs. After each increasing high, the fall that followed seemed to take him lower and lower. I feared he would try to take his own life if the drugs didn't take him first. Nausea would take over as I climbed the stairs that led to our bedrooms. Would he be lying there dead this time? Would I be the first to see him? There was always fear.

But it wasn't just fear, there were the many other ways my brother's choices affected our lives. There was the complete lack of trust from the many times he would lie to and steal from all of us. Despite the fact my father was a doctor, there were times when finances were tight due to the tremendous expense of different treatments my brother went through. And any time something special was going on, it always seemed my brother would go off on one of his binges leaving all of the worry and focus on him and taking away the happiness of the moment. The list could go on and on.

Who would have dreamed a few good kids experiencing their first buzz with a little beer at 13 would be the start of a lifelong addiction that would shatter hopes and dreams and destroy a happy family. I hope you understand that when you choose to do drugs, it's not a choice that just affects you. This can affect all those around you. And you will never know if you are the type to become addicted and lose your ability to stop until it is too late. My brother never thought he would be the one that would become addicted to drugs, but he did.

Please, don't make the same mistake he made by thinking you can drink a couple of beers and smoke a few cigarettes and then give it all up. For many people it doesn't work that way, and it's not worth the risk.

**It's your choice as to whether
you will use drugs,
but you don't have a choice
as to what the drugs will do to you.**

Chapter 6

Tobacco – America's #1 Killer

Smoking has been associated with many famous people throughout history. Winston Churchill in history books with a big cigar clutched between his lips. James Dean sporting a leather jacket with a cigarette dangling from his mouth. And then there was Andrew "Dice" Clay spouting jokes in a cloud of cigarette smoke. Johnny Carson was a two-pack-a-day guy and suffered with emphysema for 15 years before dying at age 79. And John Wayne smoked four to five packs a day before dying from lung cancer.

But chances are your most vivid memories of someone smoking was one or both of your parents. And road trips with mom and dad were the worst with all that smoke pouring into the backseat!

Step Back in Time

Tobacco has played a major role in America throughout the last two hundred years. For many years smoking was seen as a normal part of life, and its place in our culture was once as common as baseball. As you browse through the following timeline, notice how the tobacco industry has cleverly marketed its products through the years.

1886 Tobacco companies introduce tobacco cards featuring great sports figures and baseball players of the day as a marketing strategy to sell tobacco products.

1909 Baseball great Honus Wagner orders American Tobacco Company to take his picture off their *Sweet Caporal* cigarette packs, fearing it will lead children to smoke. The resulting shortage makes the Honus

Wagner card the most valuable trading card of all time selling for $1.27 million on eBay in 2005.

1913 RJ Reynolds introduces *Camel*, considered by historians to be the first modern cigarette.

1921 The phrase, "I'd walk a mile for a Camel," is coined when RJ Reynolds launches an $8 million advertising campaign.

1940's–1960's Cigarette manufacturers are one of the first industries to sponsor and advertise on television. One scene in "I Love Lucy" features Desi asking Lucy for a cigarette. Lucy fetches the Phillip Morris for him and replies, "See how easy it is to keep your man happy."

1964 "Come to where the flavor is. Come to Marlboro Country" features a cowboy known as the Marlboro Man.

1968 "You've come a long way baby." Philip Morris introduces this campaign in an effort to capture women smokers.

1971 "Winston tastes good like a cigarette should." RJ Reynolds uses the slogan in connection with race cars.

1971 Cigarette advertising is permanently banned from television in January.

1972 R.J. Reynolds becomes a major sponsor of NASCAR as an advertising mechanism for its Winston brand of cigarette, thus the "Winston Cup" series and championship.

1987 Joe Camel hits the scene and captures the attention of kids across the country, resulting in significant increase in cigarettes sales to minors.

1989 Phillip Morris Tobacco Company sponsors The Marlboro Grand Prix allowing the Marlboro brand name to appear on television for 93 minutes, thus subverting the 1971 ban on TV advertising.

1991 The *Journal of the American Medical Association* publishes two startling facts:

(1) 91percent of six-year-olds recognized Joe Camel as easily as Mickey Mouse.

(2) Since Joe Camel's introduction four years earlier, Camel's share in the under-18 (illegal) market of cigarette sales rose from 0.5 percent to 32.8 percent, amounting to over a $400-million-per-year increase.

1995 The Marlboro cowboy dies of lung cancer.

1997 The tobacco industry agrees to a historic settlement to pay $368 billion in health- related damages

1997 Joe Camel is forced into retirement by the Federal Trade Commission because of his great appeal to children.

2003 R.J. Reynolds withdraws from NASCAR sponsorship in the wake of U.S. legislation restricting avenues for tobacco advertising.[1]

The Tobacco War

Smoking played a large role in the lives of millions in the first half of the 1900's. Almost everyone smoked, and no one considered it a health risk. In fact, in the '30's and '40's, the tobacco industry actually ran ads in the *Journal of American Medical Association (JAMA)*.

But in the 1950's the tobacco industry experienced a major setback when smoking was scientifically linked to lung cancer and emphysema. Another immense setback occurred in the '60's when tobacco was linked to heart disease and fetal abnormalities. In 1966, the Surgeon General of the United States made a formal warning to Americans about the dangers of smoking. Today, all packs of cigarettes are stamped with the following statement:

INVOLVED: Parents' Connection to Drug Prevention

> **WARNING:** Smoking causes lung cancer, heart disease, emphysema, and may complicate pregnancy.

Despite the warning labels, tobacco still continues to be a serious health problem. In 1971, when the tobacco industry was banned from television commercials, the manufacturers put more emphasis on advertising to young people. The tobacco industry is well aware that the younger they can get a person hooked on tobacco the more money they make.

Terence Sullivan, a sales rep for RJ Reynolds, admitted the tobacco industry was targeting children when he was quoted as saying: "We were targeting kids, and I said at the time it was unethical and maybe illegal, but I was told it was just company policy." Sullivan later said someone once asked him who the young people were that RJR was targeting. Were they going after junior high kids or younger? Sullivan's reply was, "They got lips? We want them."[2]

The concept of targeting kids supposedly changed in 1998 when the tobacco industry promised they would no longer target youth. Despite the strict rules and regulations, the tobacco industry now spends an all-time high of $15.1 BILLION a YEAR ... that's $41 MILLION EVERYDAY on advertising.[3] Most of their focus is in convenience stores and magazines.

Although the tobacco industry swears their marketing isn't geared toward kids, a recent survey showed kids are almost twice as likely as adults to recall tobacco advertising.[4] And the large majority of smokers ages 12 to 17 prefer Marlboro, Camel and Newport, which happen to be three of the most heavily advertised brands.

Teens and Tobacco

In an effort to protect young people from the dangers of tobacco, the government has ruled it is against the law for anyone under the age of 18 to obtain or use tobacco. Despite all the efforts to protect young people from the health risks associated with tobacco, about 4,000 kids a day between the age of 12 and 17 try their first cigarette. And of that

4,000, over 1,000 young people in that age group become regular smokers everyday in the U.S.[5] More than 5 million of today's young people under the age of 18 will die prematurely because they decided to start smoking cigarettes as a teenager.[6] This is why government warnings state:

> **It's against the law for anyone under the age of 18 to obtain or use tobacco.**

The Dangers of Cigarettes

There are over **4,000 hazardous chemical compounds** in cigarettes and at least **43 are known to cause cancer**.[7] With each puff, thousands of hazardous chemicals make their way into the lungs, hearts and other vital organs.

The following are the primary causes of death in the U.S., as reported in the *Journal of American Medical Association:*

Top Eight Causes of Death in the U.S.[8]

#8	Illicit use of drugs	17,000
#7	Sexual behavior	20,000
#6	Firearms	29,000
#5	Motor vehicle accidents	43,000
#4	Influenza & pneumonia	75,000
#3	Alcohol consumption	85,000
#2	Poor diet & physical inactivity	400,000
#1	Tobacco	435,000

That's right. Tobacco is the leading cause of death in America. It's also the single most preventable cause of premature death in this country.[9] It is responsible for more than one in every five deaths in America. In fact, **more people die from tobacco use than from murders, suicide, car accidents, AIDS, heroin and cocaine combined**.[10] Even the Vice-President of Philip Morris, David Davies, has stated, "Everyone making decisions about smoking needs to understand that smoking causes disease and is addictive... There is no safe cigarette..."[11] And he's right. Not even low-tar cigarettes or any other tobacco product is considered safe.

What You Can Get From Smoking

Whether young people are lured into smoking because of curiosity, rebellion, peer pressure or they're just striving to achieve adult status, they need to realize there's a good chance they will get far more than they bargained for.

> **One in every two lifelong smokers will die from a smoking related disease.**[12]

Smoking can harm almost every organ in the body and has been documented as causing:

Heart Disease

Atherosclerotic Peripheral Vascular Disease
caused by plaque in the arteries around your heart

Cerebrovascular Disease
causes strokes

Chronic Obstructive Pulmonary Disease
chronic lung disorders causing obstruction in the airways

Intrauterine Growth Retardation
can result in an unborn baby being severely underweight

Cancer of the Lungs
one of the largest organs in the body used to breathe oxygen from air

Cancer of the Larynx or Voice Box
area of the throat containing the vocal cords – also used for breathing, swallowing, and talking

Cancer of the Esophagus
the muscular tube that carries food into the stomach

Cancer of the Urinary Bladder
the organ that collects urine

Smoking Also Contributes to Cancers of the:

Pancreas
the gland that produces and secretes digestive juices

Kidneys
the organs that filter wastes from the blood

Cervix
the opening of a woman's uterus or womb

And the Hits Just Keep on Coming

As if the preceding list wasn't bad enough, smokers are at a far greater risk than non-smokers for such problems as back and neck pain, Crohns disease, Graves disease, depression, type-2 diabetes, stomach ulcers and angina.

Smokers are also more likely to have an increased risk of cataracts, macular degeneration, hearing loss and impotence.

The Scoop on Smoking

Although most people see smoking as something reserved for adults only, it certainly doesn't start out that way! Ninety percent of all adult smokers began smoking while they were kids. No doubt most were confident they could stop anytime. However, nearly two-thirds of all teen smokers are addicted to cigarettes by the time they leave high school.[13]

> **Those who never smoke as a kid will probably NEVER become a smoker!**

If you have ever tried to smoke a cigarette, then you know the experience for a beginner smoker is usually unpleasant. The first few times a person lights up he typically feels dizzy and sick to his stomach. This is an indication the poisonous chemicals and nicotine have reached his brain and central nervous system. Obviously, the brain is trying to send a strong message. But unfortunately, the body will adjust to the adverse reaction; and soon the smoker will begin to enjoy a sense of added energy and the relaxed feeling he gets from the nicotine.

Once the smoker has inhaled, it only takes about 10 seconds for the nicotine to reach his brain.[14] With each puff, additional doses of nicotine spread throughout the brain and central nervous system. But the positive effects don't last long. In between cigarettes, the pleasures of smoking are replaced with a sense of frustration and irritability that drives the smoker to think, "I *need* another cigarette!" It's this intense desire to maintain the positive effects that causes many smokers to consume one to two packs a day. Why else would employees stand outside the workplace in the freezing cold or blazing heat puffing away on cigarettes? They *need* their nicotine fix!

If the smoker tries to quit, he quickly learns how difficult it is to break the habit. **Nearly 35 million smokers make a serious attempt to stop smoking every year, but less than seven percent are successful at kicking their addiction.**[15] Cigarettes are addictive. In fact, many believe tobacco is as addictive as heroin.

Cigars

Popularity of cigars is on the rise. However, there are some major differences in smoking cigarettes and cigars. According to the American Cancer Society, a cigar typically contains between 5 and 17 grams of tobacco, whereas one cigarette contains less than a gram of tobacco. One large cigar can have as much nicotine as an entire pack of cigarettes. It may take one to two hours to smoke a cigar, but less than 10 minutes to smoke a cigarette.

The major difference in smoking a cigarette and a cigar is how they are used. While a cigarette smoker may smoke a pack of cigarettes a day, the large majority of cigar smokers are considered occasional smokers – meaning they smoke less than one cigar a day. Those who smoke cigarettes nearly always inhale the smoke; cigar smokers seldom inhale.

This does not mean cigars are not addicting. They can be. And it doesn't mean they are not dangerous to a person's health. They are. In fact, those who smoke cigars have higher rates of various types of cancer including cancer of the lungs, lips, tongue, mouth, throat, esophagus and larynx than nonsmokers, but not as high as the rates of cigarette smokers.

Smokeless Tobacco

Over 15 percent of high school students have used smokeless tobacco – also known as chewing tobacco, chew, chaw, spit tobacco, dip and plug.[16] Smokeless tobacco comes in two forms: chewing tobacco and snuff.

As with smoking, smokeless tobacco users must first overcome the taste and sick feeling that follows the first few experiences. For those who are able to adjust to the adverse reaction, attractive side effects will soon follow. Just *a pinch between your cheek and gum* will provide increased energy and alertness, while providing a decrease in a person's appetite and stress level. However, it's important not to confuse the term smokeless with harmless because there's nothing harmless about smokeless tobacco.

The nicotine in one dip is equal to 3 or 4 cigarettes. The juice produced from smokeless tobacco is absorbed directly into the tissue of the mouth. And within 20 minutes of contact to the skin, nicotine causes stress on the heart as it increases the heart rate and blood pressure.[17] Smokeless tobacco also causes bad breath, stained teeth, increased tooth decay along with nasty sores and white patches in the mouth that can become cancerous. In other words, it doesn't matter if the tobacco is smoked, chewed or placed inside the cheek, it can still lead to death from cancer and heart disease.

This happened incredibly fast for one of my *(Todd)* co-workers. I always remember him with a dip in his cheek. The news that he had cancer of the mouth came as a shock to everyone, including his teenage son. The doctors first removed a part of his jaw, then his tongue. But even that couldn't stop the cancer, and he died several months after his first diagnosis. He hadn't even reached his 40th birthday.

There is Good News

Smoking by young people (8th – 12th grade) has declined substantially over the last ten years. Current daily smoking by 12th graders fell by half, and the drop was more than half among students in 8th and 10th grades. That means tens of thousands fewer teenage smokers![18]

Several forces are responsible for the decline in smoking among today's youth. Take another look at the timeline at the beginning of this chapter, and you will see what likely started this impressive decline. The public debate on the hazards of smoking and the questionable practices of the tobacco industry generated a great deal of media attention, which led up to the historic **Tobacco Settlement in 1997**. This trickled down to our youth and increased their perception that smoking was harmful. As a result of the settlement, big changes were made in the way the tobacco companies did business. To cover the costs of the settlement, cigarette prices rose considerably, which most studies agree means less underage buyers. The Joe Camel campaign and all billboard advertising for tobacco products ended. Settlement monies were also used to launch successful national and local anti-tobacco advertising campaigns. All of these factors play a major role in reducing the number of teenage smokers.

However, today the heated debate and many of the anti-tobacco initiatives are gone, and the impact on teenage smokers is apparent. The large decline in teenage smoking has leveled off, and it is important parents don't become immune to the on-going hazards. We must make sure our youth continue to understand the dangers of tobacco.

If you are a parent who smokes, one of the most important things you can do for yourself and your children is to quit smoking. Of course, that is no easy task! I (Todd) watched my mother struggle to quit smoking for many years as I was growing up. And although it took her several attempts, she has not had a cigarette for twenty years.

The potential dangers of secondhand smoke are of great concern. Recent government reports state that secondhand smoke contains about 50 cancer-causing chemicals and increases the risk of heart disease and lung cancer for non-smokers. The reports also state that secondhand smoke causes sudden infant death syndrome (SIDS), respiratory problems, ear infections and asthma attacks in infants and children.[19]

As a police officer (Todd), the nature of my job takes me inside many homes. At least several times a week I walk into a house or an apartment where one or more adults are smoking near young children. Sometimes the cigarette smoke is so thick I have to ask to move outside because it is hard for me to breathe during the short time I am there. Imagine what it must be like for those children to constantly breathe in that smoke while they are playing, eating and sleeping inside their home!

Studies show that parental behavior has strong influences on children. A study was done of two- to-six-year-old children role-playing in a miniature grocery store to observe the children's shopping habits. It is not surprising that children were more likely to buy cigarettes if their parents were smokers.[20]

If you are a smoker, maybe you've never tried to quit smoking, or maybe you've tried but failed. Whichever category you fit in, please keep trying until you're successful. The benefits to you and your children's health are priceless. In the coming pages you will find some ideas to help you with your decision to quit. Your personal struggle to quit is also a great opportunity to share with your children why it is so important they never start! You have first-hand experience about experimenting, building up tolerance and addiction. Our kids don't expect us to be perfect; they just want us to be honest with them.

INVOLVED: Parents' Connection to Drug Prevention

The Parent Connection

Ideas to Help You Protect Your Child From Drugs

Let's Talk About Tobacco

Most teens eventually regret their decision to start smoking. And whether they try to stop as a teen or as an adult, they typically find there isn't anything easy about giving up this addiction. Consider the familiar words of Mark Twain:

> "To cease smoking is the easiest thing I ever did;
> I ought to know because I have done it a thousand times"
>
> *Mark Twain*

Did you know most drug use begins with tobacco? It's critical children learn about the dangers of tobacco starting at an early age. Your child needs to know it's easier to say no to that first tobacco experience than to try to stop using it after the addiction has occurred. So the next tip on the Parent Connection to Drug Prevention is:

Tip # 6 on DRUG PREVENTION

Teach Your Child Your Values on Tobacco

TRY THIS IDEA!

10 Reasons to Say No to Tobacco

Share the following points with your child to help him understand why tobacco use isn't a smart choice.

1. It's against the law for anyone under the age of 18 to obtain or use tobacco.
2. Tobacco use can result in serious health problems including heart attacks, strokes, breathing problems and cancer.
3. More than 5 million of today's young people under the age of 18 will eventually die prematurely because they started smoking cigarettes as a teenager.
4. All tobacco products are dangerous. The nicotine in one dip of chewing tobacco is equal to three to four cigarettes.
5. More people die from tobacco use than from murder, suicide, car accidents, AIDS, heroin and cocaine combined.
6. Most teens who smoke regret their decision; and despite numerous efforts to quit, can't kick the habit.
7. Nearly 35 million smokers make a serious attempt to stop smoking every year, but less than seven percent are successful at kicking their addiction.
8. Teens who use tobacco are more likely to use alcohol and drugs, carry weapons, attempt suicide and engage in sexual activity than teens who don't use tobacco.
9. People who smoke have hair, breath, clothes, homes and cars that stink.
10. Those who never smoke as a teen will probably NEVER become a smoker!

HERE ARE SOME MORE IDEAS

What's in a Cigarette?

There are over 4,000 chemical compounds identified in tobacco smoke. Of these, at least 43 are known to cause cancer. Some of the more recognizable agents rolled up in a cigarette are listed below:

- Arsenic: Found in rat poison
- Acetone: Found in some nail polish remover
- Ammonia: A household cleaner
- Benzene: Rubber cement
- Carbon Monoxide: A poisonous gas
- Formaldehyde: Used to embalm dead bodies
- Hydrazine: Used in rocket fuel
- Nitrogen Oxide: A poisonous gas
- Nicotine: Substance in tobacco that causes addiction
- Tar: The agent which transports many of these chemicals directly into the body resulting in a sticky mass in the lungs. Tar also causes a dirty, yellow stain on fingers, teeth, clothes and furniture.

Note: A smoker who smokes one to three packs of cigarettes a day collects 1 to 1½ pounds of gooey, black, tar-like material in his lungs each year.

Using Everyday Experiences

The next time you and your child are walking out of the mall and you see several people lined up outside the entrance puffing on their cigarettes, take the opportunity to ask your child:

- Why do you suppose all those people are standing outside on such a hot (cold, windy, rainy etc.) day?
- What do you think their cars smell like?
- How would you like to kiss someone with stinky, smoker's breath?

Tobacco: America's #1 Killer

TRY THIS IDEA!
You Do the Math

Give your child the following math problems to solve:

1. If a 15-year-old smokes a pack of cigarettes everyday at a cost of $4.29 a pack, how much will he spend during a year?

   Have your child do the math, but the correct answer is $1,565.85.

   Question: Can you think of more exciting ways to spend $1,565.85 a year instead of letting it go up in smoke?

2. If the same 15-year-old continues to smoke one pack of cigarettes a day for the next 50 years at the average cost of $4.29 per pack, how much money will go up in smoke during the 50 years?

   Again, have your child do the math, but the correct answer is $78,292.50. (Assumes 365 days per year.)

3. If you take into account two percent inflation over 50 years, how much money will go up in smoke?

   The answer is $132,438.66. (Assumes 365 days per year.)

4. If a 15-year-old smokes one pack of cigarettes a day for 50 years at the rate of $4.29 a day, exactly how smart is he?

5. Let's say instead of spending $4.29 a day on cigarettes, he decides to put the money into high-quality mutual funds or individual stocks earning 8 percent. How much money will he have by age 65?

INVOLVED: Parents' Connection to Drug Prevention

If your child is old enough to do the math, have him work out the problem. If not, just tell him the correct answer is $898,438.00. A pretty hefty retirement! Not only will he have almost a million dollars to enjoy because of his decision to say NO to tobacco, he'll have a much greater chance of having good health to enjoy life when he's older.

Suggestions on How to Quit Smoking

Almost all smokers will agree it's not easy to quit smoking. Few are successful, especially the first few times they attempt to quit. Go over the following suggestions on how to quit smoking with your child. Assuming she's not a smoker, it might help her decide to never start smoking. If she is a smoker, maybe it will encourage her to stop. If you are a smoker, this list may be helpful to you and also give you the chance to share with your child what you will have to do to be successful. As you go through the list, try asking questions such as, "Why do you think it would be necessary to throw all your cigarettes, ash trays and lighters away? Doesn't that sound a little extreme?"

- Be determined!
- Set a date to stop.
- Throw all your cigarettes, lighters and ash trays away.
- Ask your friends not to smoke around you.
- Don't drink alcohol – it destroys self-control.
- Tell others you are quitting so they can support you.
- Be prepared to feel irritable, depressed and gain a few pounds, but know this will pass.
- Stay busy with activities you enjoy so boredom won't sidetrack your resolve.
- Plan a reward system. Tell yourself that if you can go one week without smoking you will reward yourself with (blank), and then plan a bigger reward to celebrate one month and then one year of being tobacco free.

- Understand you cannot take even one puff of a cigarette or you'll be hooked again.
- Consider nicotine replacement therapy using nicotine gum, patch, inhaler or nasal spray. Some of these are available over-the-counter and some by prescription only.
- Consider behavioral therapy by seeing a therapist who specializes in tobacco addiction. The therapist will recommend ways to conquer cravings as well as provide emotional support and help in identifying triggers (stress, smell of smoke, boredom, ashtrays and lighters, etc.)
- Use a combination of the treatments listed above to increase your chances of successfully quitting for good!

References

[1] Clinimmune Labs, March 29, 2003. www.uchsc.edu/sm/cihl/history_of_cigarette_smoke.htm
[2] P. J. Hilts, *Smokescreen: The Truth Behind the Tobacco Industry Cover-Up*, (Addison Wesley Publishing Co., 1996), p. 96-98.
[3] Campaign for Tobacco-Free Kids, 2004.
[4] International Communications Research (ICR), *National Telephone Survey of Teens Aged 12 to 17 and Adults*, March 2007.
[5] Centers for Disease Control and Prevention, *Smoking & Tobacco Use: Fact Sheet*, December 2006.
[6] Centers for Disease Control and Prevention, *Tobacco Information and Prevention Source: Teens and Tobacco Facts Not Fiction*, April 2003.
[7] Centers for Disease Control and Prevention, *Reducing Tobacco Use: A Report of the Surgeon General*, August 2000.
[8] Ali H. Mokdad, PhD, et al., *Journal of the American Medical Association*, (JAMA), 291(10)2004, "Actual Causes of Death in the U.S. 2000," pp. 1230-1246.
[9] Centers for Disease Control and Prevention, *Chronic Disease Prevention – Targeting Tobacco Use: The Nation's Leading Cause of Preventable Death At a Glance*, May 2007.
[10] Centers for Disease Control and Prevention, *Health Effects of Cigarette Smoking Fact Sheet*, February 2004.
[11] Action on Smoking and Health (ASH), Extracts from a Interview with David Davies, VP, Philip Morris International on "Hard Talk", *BBC News*, March 2001.
[12] Action on Smoking and Health, *Factsheet #2 Smoking Statistics: Illness and Death*, 2006.
[13] Campaign for Tobacco-Free Kids, *Med Gallegly: Smoking*, March 2, 2007.
[14] National Institute on Drug Abuse, "Nicotine: What the Research Shows," *Colorado Prevention News*, Autumn 2002,3:1.
[15] Ibid.
[16] National Institute on Drug Abuse, *Monitoring the Future*, May 2008.
[17] Centers for Disease Control and Prevention, *Spit Tobacco: Dip, Chew, Snuff, Smokeless*, July 23, 2003.
[18] National Institute on Drug Abuse. *Monitoring the Future*, May 2008.
[19] U.S. Surgeon General's Press Release, *New Surgeon General's Report Focuses on the Effects of Secondhand Smoke*, June 2006.
[20] Madeline A. Dalton, et al., Use of Cigarettes and Alcohol by Preschoolers While Role-playing as Adults "Honey, Have Some Smokes," *Arch Pediatr Adolesc Med.* 2005:159:854-859.

Chapter 7

Alcohol –
The Most Acceptable Drug

If you've had heart-to-heart talks with your children about drugs, no doubt you've discussed drugs such as marijuana, ecstasy and cocaine. But have you discussed alcohol?

It's surprising how many adults have a hard time thinking of alcohol as a drug. Perhaps it's because alcohol can be legally consumed by those over 21. Therefore, to call a beer or a glass of wine or a scotch on the rocks a drug just doesn't seem to fit. There's also the possibility many of those who do enjoy an alcoholic beverage now and then (or on a regular basis) are just uncomfortable calling what they're consuming a drug. However, alcohol can change a person's behavior and can be addictive. Therefore, alcohol meets the definition of a drug.

Consider these facts:

- By the end of high school, almost three out of four students (72 percent) have consumed alcohol.[1]

- More than half (55 percent) of high school seniors and almost one in five (18 percent) of eighth graders have been *drunk*.[2]

- 92 percent of 12th graders state that alcohol is easy to obtain.[3]

- 65 percent of children ages 10 to 18 report obtaining their alcohol from family and friends.[4]

Whether you have a few beers left over from the weekend barbeque or a fully-stocked liquor cabinet, that alcohol is easily accessible to curious kids looking for their first buzz – or for the more experienced teen, a chance to get wasted. Although alcohol is socially acceptable among most adults and legal for all those over 21 – it is *not* legal for our children.

> **It's against the law in all 50 states for a person under the age of 21 to consume alcohol.**

What's the Harm?

Perhaps you enjoy a beer when you get home from work. Maybe a glass of wine at dinner relaxes you after a long, hard day. And maybe you're scratching your head and asking yourself, "What's the harm in kids experimenting a little here and there with alcohol? They're just having fun."

But don't forget: you are an adult who is, hopefully, fully capable of knowing your limits. Yet a teenager consuming alcohol is far different from an adult. First of all, teens don't drink to relax. They drink to get drunk. They and their friends want to experience the feeling of going wild and doing crazy things totally over the edge.

It's also important to note that since a teenager's body is not fully developed, alcohol can have far more adverse affects on them than on adults. And in most cases, it takes far less alcohol to intoxicate a teenager than an adult.

Consider this possible scenario:

> It's Friday night, and your 14-year-old daughter is at a sleepover with a few of her friends. It appears, however, she neglected to inform you that the parents of the girl hosting the sleepover are out-of-town. Neither did she reveal that this particular house comes equipped with a fully stocked bar.
>
> As your daughter begins to drink that evening, the alcohol is quickly absorbed into the lining of her stomach. This

Alcohol: The Most Acceptable Drug

may irritate her stomach and cause her to feel queasy. With enough alcohol, her stomach may launch a full-force attack and cause extreme vomiting.

From the lining of her stomach, the alcohol quickly enters her bloodstream. All the functions of her central nervous system begin to slow as the alcohol affects her brain and every other organ in her body.

Her behavior begins to change as she starts doing things she would never consider doing without the alcohol. Her vision blurs, her speech slurs. She stumbles and falls to the ground. Of course, this only causes your daughter and all her friends to laugh and giggle as they consume more alcohol.

I can hear some of you saying as you read this story, "So what? Who cares if a few girls sneak around and get a little tipsy from drinking some alcohol? Kids do crazy things."

Oh – did I neglect to mention it wasn't just girls at the sleep over? ... Let's continue with the story.

It's 8:00 o'clock on that same Friday night. Sam's parents realize a six-pack of beer is missing from the refrigerator in their garage. They laugh at the fact that their 16-year-old son thinks he can sneak beer out of their house and then go to a sleepover with two of his buddies without his parents noticing. They talk about whether they should confront their son, ground him or just let it go. After a lengthy discussion, they assure each other this is just another phase their son is going through and agree the less they make of it the better. Besides, how much harm can a six pack of beer cause three boys?

It's true. Two beers throughout the evening per boy probably won't do these guys serious harm. But there were a number of additional questions Sam's parents should have asked before they decided to blow this off as a whimsical, boys-will-be-boys situation. Let's continue.

INVOLVED: Parents' Connection to Drug Prevention

Around 10:30, Sam's mother walks into the den where she finds her husband soundly sleeping in his comfortable chair. The TV is blaring. She mutes the TV and wakes her husband. She tells him she's been thinking more about the missing beer, and she just isn't comfortable with the situation. She then asks her husband, "Are we sure the one six pack of beer is all the three will drink tonight? How do we know the other boys aren't bringing additional alcoholic beverages or other drugs to the sleepover? What if the six pack of beer is what Sam plans to consume, and the other boys are bringing their own alcohol. What if they decide to drive somewhere after they consume the alcohol? Come to think of it, how do we even know Sam's really over at Andrew's house?"

The father shrugs his shoulders and says, "If it will make you feel better, call Andrew's mom and make sure the boys are okay."

It's almost midnight when your phone awakens you from a deep sleep. The voice on the other end is a familiar one. It's the mother of one of your daughter's best friends. She's asking you to join her at the house where the girls are having their sleepover. She says the details she received are sketchy, but she does know everyone at the sleepover is drunk – including three older boys.

You're suddenly hit with a mix of emotions – confusion, anger and fear for what your daughter may have experienced over the past six hours since leaving your home, not to mention what the future might hold.

Unfortunately, many parents can identify with situations similar to these.

Acquiring a Taste

For many people, young and old alike, alcohol is an acquired taste. Perhaps that's why so many teens, especially girls, are turning to the sugary, alcoholic drinks known as Alco-pop. Drinks such as

Alcohol: The Most Acceptable Drug

Smirnoff Ice, Bacardi Silver and Mike's Hard Lemonade are appealing to teens because the fruit flavored alcohol drinks taste more like flavored soda-pop than alcoholic beverages. But don't be fooled. These 12-fluid-ounce bottles have about the same, or in some cases even more, alcohol content than most of the leading brands of beer. These girly drinks may be a significant factor in why more teenage girls start drinking alcohol each year than guys. Of course, these sweet-flavored drinks can easily pave the way for stronger drugs such as marijuana, cocaine and heroin.

I (Marilyn) speak to thousands of students in metropolitan cities and small towns every year. A common thread running through all communities is that kids love to party! The term "love to party" tends to be code for "we love to get drunk."

Recently a ninth-grade girl told me, "It's fun to get drunk because then you can do insane things – like you don't even care who you hook-up with. And the great thing is you don't remember half the stuff you did the next day." ("Hook-up" is the term for having sex with no strings attached.)

Alcohol is the #1 drug of choice among America's youth.[5]

A can of beer has about as much alcohol as a 1.5 ounce shot of liquor, a 5 ounce glass of wine or a wine cooler.

Binge Drinking

As previously stated, teens don't drink to relax – they drink to get drunk. Excessive drinking is called binge drinking, which refers to five or more drinks in one sitting. **The large majority of teens who drink today are binge drinkers.**[6] Males report a slightly higher rate of binge drinking than females, but the differences are rapidly diminishing.

Anytime a teen drinks alcohol, the risk factors of other risky behaviors go up. But when teens *binge* drink, the risk factors go up significantly. This includes increased risk of smoking cigarettes, engaging in sexual activity, becoming a victim of date rape, fighting, riding with a drunk driver, using other illegal drugs and attempting suicide.

Binge drinking can lead to alcohol poisoning, which can cause violent vomiting. The person might also experience extreme sleepiness or become unconscious. There can be difficulty in breathing followed by seizures. In extreme cases, the person can die.

Drinking and Depression

For years many experts assumed depressed teens turn to alcohol, drugs and sex to self-medicate the pain of their depression. However, a recent two-year study of 13,000 middle school and high-school-aged students found the opposite to be true. The study indicates that depression is significantly increased *after* girls start experimenting with low levels of alcohol, drugs and/or sexual activity. Depression is significantly increased for boys *after* they start using high levels of alcohol, drugs and/or sexual experimentation. [7] In other words, depression came after the alcohol, drugs and/or sex.

Drinking, drug use, sex and depression are not exactly the activities most parents want to use when describing their teenagers, especially considering the majority of teen suicide victims have a history of depression, sexual activity and/or alcohol and drug abuse.

Girls Get Drunk Easier Than Guys

When a guy and girl of equal weights drink the same amount of alcohol, the girl will typically feel the effects more than the guy. The reason is because females have a lower percentage of body water and enzyme activity that breaks down alcohol in their system compared to guys. Therefore, alcohol is more concentrated in the girl's body and more diluted in the guy's body. As a result, the girl will typically feel the effects of the alcohol more than the guy. Chances are she will also have greater difficulty in thinking, making decisions, reaction time, eye-hand coordination as well as greater problems with short- and long-term memory loss.

Drinking and Driving

Teenagers are risk-takers. Therefore, the risk of automobile crashes significantly goes up when a teen is behind the wheel. Teens enjoy impressing their friends while driving. They have less experience behind the wheel. They like to speed. They're easily distracted. They don't like to wear seat belts. Add alcohol to the mix, and the chances of a disaster occurring sky rockets! That's why **motor vehicle crashes are the leading cause of death among U.S. teens.**[8]

FACT:
- Every 31 minutes a person in the U.S. is killed in an alcohol-related traffic accident.[9]
- Every two minutes a person is injured in an alcohol-related traffic accident.[10]

While those statistics are troubling, they were far worse not long ago. In the early 1990's, a person was killed in an alcohol-related traffic accident every 15 minutes. Fortunately, public education, changes in attitude and stricter punishment for drunk driving has reduced the number of deaths. Education and continued enforcement works!

Not long ago I (Todd) attended an alcohol-awareness program at a local high school. A *mock* DUI crash was staged using real cars and students from the school. As the juniors and seniors walked to the bleachers to see firsthand the events that unfold at a crash scene, many laughed as they saw their friends hanging out of the car windows and lying in the street. Others saw the enactment as an opportunity to escape their next class. The sirens of the arriving police cars and medical teams drowned out the laughter and discussion in the bleachers. As firemen used the Jaws of Life to extricate a student "victim" and officers arrested the student "drunk driver," the kids watching couldn't help but be drawn into the reality of the situation.

The Flight-for-Life helicopter landed close by and airlifted out the critically injured student, and the drunk driver was driven away in a police car. A short time later an announcement was made over the loud speaker that the student airlifted out died while en route to the hospital. He was only 17-years-old. As I witnessed the program unfold I noticed laughter being replaced by sorrow. Many students embraced one another, and some cried uncontrollably at the thought of losing a friend in the accident. Although this was nothing more than a staged drama, for a brief moment in time the students understood the destructive power of alcohol. I have seen my share of real accidents just like the one I have described above. Yet, I can honestly tell you I was just as moved as many of the students that day!

Unfortunately, few high-school students will have the opportunity to witness such a prevention program. That is why it is so important for parents to be heavily *involved* in educating their children about the danger of drinking and driving.

> **The peak hours of drunk driving are between 1:00 a.m. and 3:00 a.m.
> when as many as one in four (25 percent) of drivers are estimated to have been drinking.**[11]

It seemed like no big deal when 20-year-old Pierre used his fake ID to get beer for his underage friends. What could be so wrong about helping a few boys have some fun? For Sean, 16, and his 15-year-old friends, Josh, Kyle, Travis, and Cody, it meant impressing their friends by showing up at the party with some booze.

Fourteen-year-old Danielle had permission from her mom to have the party at her house that night. When Sean and his friends showed up with alcohol, Danielle got upset and told her mother. The mom threatened to call the police on several occasions before the boys finally left.

Sean drove away from the party with his four friends. No doubt they were having the time of their life. Perhaps they were even feeling invincible as Sean drove in excess of 80 mph through the 25 mph residential zone. But sadly, no one is invincible!

Alcohol: The Most Acceptable Drug

Sean lost control of the car, rammed into a cinder-block wall; and everything came to a screeching halt. Josh, Kyle and Travis were killed in the accident; Cody was seriously injured. Blood tests showed Sean's blood alcohol level was 0.19 percent, more than twice the legal limit for adults in Nevada. The three dead boys all had alcohol levels above the legal limit as well.

The consequences of Sean's actions have left him with the pain and guilt of knowing he killed his three childhood friends. The everyday pressures of growing up are difficult enough, but to face such a heavy burden at such a young age is tragic. The three boys' parents only have the memory of the sons they will never see again. Birthdays will be met with grief and sadness instead of a joyous celebration. So many lives have been left reeling in the wake of this tragedy.

(Todd) That accident was only about one mile from my house. My sons and I drove past the makeshift memorial for several weeks. It was a sad and harsh reminder of how life can change in the blink of an eye.

Additional Problems

The problems of teenagers and alcohol go beyond broken bones, mutilated bodies and death. When teens drink, one of the first things they lose is their self-control. After only one or two drinks, two good kids from good homes can find themselves letting go and letting their hormones take over. The next thing they know, they're having sex.

There's a good chance their actions have little or nothing to do with being in love. Chances are they're just hooking-up. But sometimes such situations result in kids sharing more than their bodies.

Casual sex among today's teens has led to an epidemic consisting of over 25 significant sexually transmitted diseases (STDs). Over 10,000 teenagers contract an STD *everyday* in America.[12] One out of every four sexually active teens gets an (STD) each year.[13] Many of these diseases have no cure, and some can last a lifetime. These diseases can be humiliating, painful and even deadly. The following is a list of the most common STDs in America and their effects:

- Chlamydia and gonorrhea can cause pain, infertility problems, premature births and tubal pregnancies.

- Herpes can cause a lifetime of recurring painful sores in the genital area.

- Human Papillomavirus (HPV) can result in embarrassing genital warts, cancer and death.

- AIDS can destroy a person's immune system and lead to death.

Don't assume condoms will protect your child. When teens drink alcohol, they're far less likely to give condoms any thought. Even if they do think to use a condom, that's no guarantee the condom will prevent the spread of STDs since condoms provide little protection from some of the leading STDs.

But let's say the two inebriated teens are fortunate and don't infect each other with diseases. That doesn't mean their hooking-up escapade was risk free. Sometimes, despite their desires to keep the relationship totally casual, the unexpected happens.

An attorney shared with me (Marilyn) just such a situation. He told me about a 16-year-old girl who went to a party one Friday night; I'll call her Rachel. After a couple of beers she was feeling pretty good. About this time an 18-year-old senior, whom I'll call Keith, walked in and proceeded to down several beers. When their eyes met, one thing led to another; and you can guess what came next.

A few weeks later, when Rachel realized she was pregnant, she knew Keith was the father of her baby. But Rachel barely knew Keith and had no desire for him to be involved in her life. She told her family and friends she had no idea who the father was.

Fast forward six years. Rachel is now a 22-year-old single mother struggling to make ends meet. She works long, hard hours as a waitress and barely has enough energy to take care of her five-year-old son – not to mention she has absolutely no social life.

It was a Saturday evening when Keith strolled into the restaurant with his cute little wife. Rachel had heard he recently returned home from college with a diploma and a new bride. Keith looked directly at Rachel as he entered the restaurant. It was obvious

Alcohol: The Most Acceptable Drug

he had no recollection of their previous encounter. Why should he? Their meeting was a drunken, one-night stand six years ago.

Rachel, on the other hand, recognized Keith immediately. As she watched the happy couple enjoy a quiet romantic dinner together, she couldn't help but think that life just wasn't fair. Here Keith was enjoying life and climbing the ladder of success. Rachel, on the other hand, was struggling to raise her son and living paycheck to paycheck.

That's when Rachel got the bright idea to get an attorney and see if there was any chance she could get Keith to start providing child support. The attorney drew up papers and served Keith with a paternity suit naming him as the father of Rachel's son.

Needless to say, Keith was livid, as well as highly embarrassed, when a stranger enters his office and serves him with legal papers. Of course, he denied the accusation and demanded a DNA test. When the results came back, Keith was shocked to find out he did indeed have a 5-year-old son.

The courts ordered Keith to pay child support until his son turns 18. But it doesn't stop there. Keith has to also make up the past five years of missed child support.

And before we leave this story, let's consider the innocent bystanders who will be greatly impacted through this ordeal. First, there will be Rachel's and Keith's son. It will be painful for him to learn one day that he was the product of two drunken teenagers who happened to hook up one night; and the only reason his dad got involved in his life was because his mother and the Court ordered him to fork over some money every month.

Then there's Keith's wife. Can you imagine the devastation she will feel when her husband announces he has a son, and a significant portion of their income will now go to care for this little boy whom neither of them knew existed?

It's amazing how a few beers and lack of self-control can have such a lasting impact on so many lives.

No Warning Label!

Just a few years ago, it seemed every media outlet was running frightening stories about a dangerous drug called GHB. It was imperative to warn girls and women of the sexual predators who were using the insidious drug as a means of incapacitating females for their own deviant sexual pleasures. Suddenly GHB-detecting stir sticks, test strips and tooth picks were being pushed as a means of protection.

I (Todd) filled many requests to give news interviews and to speak at community awareness programs to educate the public about the serious threat the little-known drug GHB posed to unsuspecting women. Many women confided how fearful they were about someone slipping the drug into their drinks when they went to clubs and bars.

Unfortunately, there are many incidents every year where women are victims of sexual assault by strangers and acquaintances who slip GHB or other drugs such as Rohypnol (pronounced row-hip-nol) and Ketamine (also known as Special K) into their drinks. However, I couldn't understand why these particular drugs created such a panic when another drug is responsible for tens of thousands more sexual assaults each year. And yet this drug has received little media coverage and few calls for community awareness programs warning the public about its dangers.

Of course, I am talking about alcohol. Unlike the **date-rape drugs**, alcohol isn't slipped into any unsuspecting woman's drinks. It is intentionally ingested! Alcoholic beverages flow freely at bars, clubs and house parties but never with the following warning label:

> **WARNING!**
> **Overindulgence of this product**
> **may lead to increased vulnerability to**
> **victimization by lurking sexual predators.**

Sure, I understand the difference. For the media, a drunken woman being sexually assaulted doesn't rise to the level of a sensational news story. But I can't comprehend why many see it less traumatic for the victim because she drank too much alcohol. All too often, victims of sexual assault are dismissed, seen as less credible and even sometimes told it was their fault for drinking too much. How would you feel if it were your daughter? Would you think she got what she deserved?

Alcohol: The Most Acceptable Drug

More than 97,000 college students are victims of alcohol-related sexual assault each year.[14] But unknown predators aren't the only ones committing all the sexual-assault crimes. Acquaintances and friends often see nothing wrong with taking advantage of a girl when she's in a drunken state. In fact, some guys have the attitude that if a girl is passed out, she's fair game.

It might be at a Friday-night party and a guy thinks to himself, "It's no big deal. I'm not going to hurt her; and besides, we've had sex together before." But we need to teach our young men consent cannot be given when someone is passed out.

Sexual contact without consent is *RAPE*.

Rape is a felony offense punishable by many years in prison. It doesn't matter whether the girl passed out after getting drunk from her own initiative or she passed out as a result of a guy encouraging her to keep drinking or because he slipped something into her drink. If he has sexual contact with her while she's unconscious, he has committed rape and could end up behind bars for many years. This is important information all men, young and old, need to know.

Not only is rape always wrong, it is also a horrible ordeal for any woman to ever experience. Rape can result in serious emotional scars and psychological problems that can last a lifetime.

Major Risk Factors

As already stated several times, the worst thing a parent can do is to be naïve and think their child would never get involved in drugs and alcohol. Any child, even a good kid from a good home, is at risk for becoming involved with drugs. Consider the major risk factors as you think through the following questions:

1. Is your child living with **stress**? All teens tend to stress out from time to time, but teens living with constant stress are more likely to turn to alcohol or drugs.
2. Is **alcohol easily accessible** for your child? This could be through your own home or your child's friends' homes.

3. Is there **opportunity** for your child to drink? For example, do your children and their friends spend lots of time unsupervised?
4. Is your child dealing with **peer pressure**? If your child's friends are drinking or using other drugs, it will be extremely difficult for him not to follow the crowd.
5. Does your child struggle with a **poor self-esteem**? Children who have a poor self-image tend to be pleasers. These young people are more likely to become involved with drugs than those with high self-esteem.
6. Is your child a **victim of abuse**? A child who has been physically or sexually abused has a greater risk of turning to alcohol.
7. Has your child **experienced a traumatic event**? Children who have dealt with trauma are more likely to become involved with alcohol than children who have not experienced trauma.
8. Does your child have a **family member with a drinking problem**? Children with an alcoholic family member (parent, sibling, grandparent, etc.) are more likely to have a drinking problem than children whose family members are not alcoholics.

A Word of Warning

People who begin drinking as teenagers are far more likely to acquire a drinking problem than those who start drinking after age 21.

> **Those who begin drinking before age 15 are four times more likely to become an alcoholic than those who began drinking after 21.**[15]

As stated earlier, addiction is a disease of the brain. For some, those early drinks seem to throw a switch in the brain that will turn off a person's stopping mechanism. What starts out as a few kids just having fun with their first buzz from booze can turn into a lifetime of addiction.

Most people who become alcoholics refuse to admit they have a problem. They usually spend a lifetime trying to cover up their drinking problem, but those closest to them are seldom fooled. Despite repeated efforts to cut back on the amount of alcohol consumed, they are seldom successful. In fact, the mark of a true alcoholic is the person who cannot control his intake. His only hope of gaining complete freedom is to never consume another drink; and that is a battle few alcoholics ever win without strong determination, lots of intervention and life-long commitment. Even if he does stop drinking, he and his family know that if he ever picks up another drink the cycle can start all over again.

The Parent Connection

Ideas to Help You Protect Your Child From Drugs

Taking a Stand

The previous chapter discussed the importance of frequently stating, "Our family does not do drugs." But since many people, teens included, don't consider alcohol to be a drug, you need to make sure your child knows where you stand on alcohol. However, before you make a declaration of no alcohol to your child, you need to carefully think where you stand on this issue.

If you NEVER consume alcohol and you are confident you never will, then you can confidently say to your child, "Our family does not use drugs or alcohol." It would be wise to explain to your child why you hold these convictions. For example, if your values are based upon religious convictions, show your children the scriptures backing your beliefs and then make sure you set the example for your child and *never* drink alcohol – ever. Because if your child happens to see you drinking or even hears of you having a glass of wine or a can of beer, you could lose all credibility. Teenagers can be harsh in their judgments and may view you as a hypocrite and liar.

However, if you enjoy an occasional mixed drink, a can of beer or glass of wine, then you need to change your phrase to "Our family does not use drugs, and we take a strong stand against under-age drinking."

Once you know where you stand on the issue of alcohol, you're ready for the next step in the Parent Connection to Drug Prevention.

Tip #7 on DRUG PREVENTION

Teach Your Child Your Values on Alcohol

Alcohol: The Most Acceptable Drug

Setting an Example

Remember, children learn far more from what they see you do than from what you say you do. Therefore, if you do drink, it is important you always drink in moderation and *never* get drunk. One of the worst things parents can do is let their children see them drunk. It will be an experience a child of any age would be hard pressed to forget – even if it only happens once or twice.

(Todd) Recalling that moment for me after all these years still brings me to tears. I remember it as if it were yesterday. I was twelve and my sister was nine. My mother had allowed us to spend a week with my father during the summer. It was the first time in many years I had time with my dad, and I was really excited.

At that point, I had never seen my dad drink, nor had I ever seen anyone drunk. But I have never forgotten the pain I felt my first time for both.

My sister and I had returned to my dad's apartment from playing at the pool. We knocked on the door several times before he finally answered. He opened the door, looked at us and said "Who the F*** are you?" When I told him we were his kids, he replied, "I don't have any kids" and slammed the door in my face. We spent that night at a neighbor's apartment. What a sad day. One I wish I could forget. Fortunately, it was the only time I ever saw my dad drunk. Maybe he realized his mistake.

It's one thing to have an occasional beer or a glass of wine and be in complete control; but when your drinking gets to the point of changing your behavior, your child will find it difficult, perhaps impossible, to respect you. There's also a good chance your child will soon follow your actions and not your words.

TRY THESE IDEAS!

10 Reasons to Avoid Alcohol

If you want your child to embrace your values, he needs to understand why you believe the way you do. Discuss the following facts and statistics as you share your values with him.

1. It's against the law in America for anyone under the age of 21 to consume alcohol.
2. One drink can cause a teen to fail a breath test. In many states an underage drinker faces the loss of driving privileges until the age of 21.
3. Every 31 minutes a person in the U.S. is killed in an alcohol-related traffic accident.[16]
4. A young person who drinks alcohol increases the risk of memory loss.
5. Teens who drink alcohol are more likely to be depressed, suffer from anxiety and consider suicide.
6. Alcohol use can cause a person to gain weight and have bad breath.
7. Drinking alcohol causes a person to lose control and increases the chance of sexual activity with one or more partners. This increases the risk of sexually transmitted diseases (STDs) and pregnancy. STDs can cause infertility problems, painful recurring sores, genital warts, cancer and death. A pregnancy can result in lost dreams and 18 years of child support.
8. Girls tend to feel the effects of alcohol easier and faster than guys. As a result, she will have greater difficulty in thinking clearly and making good decisions. If a girl passes out from alcohol, she is in danger of being raped. If a guy has sex with a girl who is passed out, he is guilty of rape and could spend many years in prison.
9. There is no way to determine who will become an alcoholic. However, people who begin drinking as teenagers are far more likely to have a drinking problem than people who start drinking after age 21.
10. There is no quick cure for alcoholism.

Alcohol: The Most Acceptable Drug

Write Your Child a Letter

After you have shared your values and the reasons for taking your stand on drugs and alcohol, put your thoughts in writing. In a personal letter, spell out your stand on drugs and alcohol. Your letter might be something like the following:

> *From the first moment I held you in my arms, you became the joy of my life. I love you more than you will ever know. As your parent, it is my responsibility to provide for you, to protect you and nurture you. As you grow up and prove your ability to make wise choices, the protective boundaries I have placed around you will begin to disappear. But one rule that will never waiver is the one concerning drugs. I will not tolerate illegal drug use, including under-age drinking. I love you and believe in you too much to watch you destroy your mind, body and future with something so destructive. I know you have the strong character necessary to stand firm and say no to drugs and alcohol and yes to a bright future.*

You might want to go so far as having this letter matted and framed and then ask your child to keep it by his or her bed at all times as a reminder of your love and expectations regarding drugs and alcohol.

Dealing with Disobedience

Let's say you tell your 15-year-old son he will lose his privileges to go out with his friends for a designated amount of time if you ever find out he is involved with drugs or alcohol. Then one night it happens. You smell alcohol on your son's breath when he comes home from a night out with his friends. You obviously have no option but to confront him. However, the way you handle the confrontation is important.

First of all, do not have your discussion with him until he's sober and you're calm. In other words, wait until the next day when you're both in a better frame of mind to have a discussion. When you confront him, your tone should be calm as you say, "I'm very disappointed you chose to go against our family's values regarding drugs last night."

Just hearing you say the words, "I'm disappointed," may be enough to change your child's behavior right there and then. Most children have an overwhelming desire to please their parents, and the thought of disappointing Mom and Dad can be devastating. But remember, you have already spelled out the consequences. Now it's time to enforce what you said – even if it means your child will miss some big, upcoming event.

Since the consequences are already outlined, there is no reason for you to give a long lecture. Besides, most kids stop listening after a couple of minutes. So anything you say after two or three minutes will basically just be you talking to yourself.

If your child starts to argue or says something like, "That's not fair!" Do not lash back or raise your voice. Otherwise, this discussion will escalate into an argument – and there is no reason to argue. Your child knew the family rule, and he knew the consequences when he broke the rule. Now all you have to do is to calmly reply, "I've told you for many years our family does NOT do drugs. You knew the rule, and you knew the consequences. I'm sorry you chose to break the rule, but now you've left me no other option but to enforce the punishment."

Then make sure you conclude the conversation by reminding him that you love him. He needs to know there is absolutely nothing he can do to cause you to stop loving him. You can do this with a gentle hug, a pat on the shoulder or simple eye-to-eye contact as you say, "Even though I'm disappointed in the decision you made last night, I still love you." At this point, drop the discussion and move on.

If your child is not remorseful, you would be wise to seek professional help from a reputable child psychologist or professional counselor. Several sessions with an individual who is trained in dealing with such issues will not only show your child how serious you are about this matter, it may also shed light on underlying issues that need to be resolved before the problems escalate.

Even if your child shows genuine remorse but comes home smelling of alcohol again, you will be wise to seek outside help. At the very least, your child is displaying signs of disrespect and disobedience; but on the other hand, this could be early signs of a serious drug problem. Either way, your child needs to know you have no intentions of ignoring the situation.

Curfews

(Todd) I have spent most of my years with the police department working the night shift. I can't recall one time where I dealt with a teenager who was out past midnight when it was a good thing. Unfortunately, I witnessed too many accident scenes where teens were injured or killed or were victims of crime after midnight.

As stated earlier, the peak hours of drunk driving are between 1:00 a.m. and 3:00 a.m. when as many as one in four (25 percent) of drivers are estimated to have been drinking.[17] In other words, even sober people cannot feel safe on the roads after midnight.

Since most parents don't stay up after midnight, teenagers may believe they can get away with whatever they please. This often includes drugs, alcohol and sex. With this in mind, it is wise to set an age-appropriate curfew for your children to assure they are home by a reasonable time. For example, you might require your 16-year-old to be home by 11:00. When he's 17, you can add an additional 30 minutes; and when he's 18, you can extend his curfew until midnight. There may be occasional exceptions when you expand the curfew for a major event; but enforcing a reasonable curfew is important and one of the best steps you can take to prevent your child from being injured, arrested, or worse. This certainly will not win you *The Most Popular Parent of the Year Award,* but allowing teens to be out after midnight is courting disaster.

HERE'S AN IDEA!

Home Movies

A mother shared with me (Marilyn) about an evening when she heard her teenage daughter come in later than her curfew allowed on Friday night. The mother got out of bed to confront her daughter about the late hour. As she watched her daughter climb the stairs toward her bedroom, she realized there were bigger problems to deal with than the broken curfew. It was obvious her daughter was drunk.

Even though the mother was extremely upset, she knew this was not the time to discuss choices and consequences of drinking alcohol. However, when she heard her daughter throwing up, she retrieved her camera and captured the next few moments on film.

The daughter was too drunk to even notice her mother standing in the doorway of the bathroom. After eventually pulling her head out of the toilet, the drunken girl slithered to the floor and fell asleep in a puddle of vomit; and meantime, mom kept the camera rolling.

The next day after the daughter had showered and dressed, the mother informed her they needed to talk about the broken curfew and the fact that she had come home inebriated. The daughter quickly apologized for coming home late and made a few flimsy excuses for her tardiness, but she totally denied being drunk.

The mother didn't say a word. She simply pushed the play button on the DVD remote. The daughter immediately knew she was busted, not to mention humiliated by her actions and appearance. That was the first and last time this young lady came home drunk. How wonderful it would be if all drug problems were so easily solved!

References

[1] National Institute on Drug Abuse, *Monitoring the Future,* April 2008.
[2] Ibid.
[3] Ibid.
[4] The Century Council by Teenage Research Unlimited (TRU), May 2003.
[5] National Institutes of Health, National Institute on Alcohol Abuse and Alcoholism, *Alcohol Alert: Underage Drinking,* January 2006.
[6] Centers for Disease Control and Prevention, "Binge Drinking is Common Among High School Students," *Media Relations Press Release,* 2007.
[7] D.D. Hallfors, et al., "Which Comes First in Adolescence – Sex and Drugs or Depression?" *American Journal of Preventive Medicine,* 2005.
[8] Centers for Disease Control and Prevention, *"Teen Drivers: Fact Sheet," Injury Center,* 2006.
[9] National Center for Statistics and Analysis, *Fatalities and Alcohol Involvement Among Drivers and Motorcycle Operators in 2005,* August 2006.
[10] Ibid.
[11] S. Levitt, J. Porter, Harvard University, National Science Foundation, 2002.
[12] Alan Guttmacher Institute, "Sexuality Education," *Facts in Brief,* July 2002.
[13] The American College of Obstetricians and Gynecologists, Committee on Adolescent Health Care, *Tool Kit for Teen Care: Sexually Transmitted Diseases,* 2003.
[14] National Institute of Health, *News in Health: Discussing Drinking – A Back-to-School Conversation You Need to Have,* 2006.
[15] B.F. Grant, D.A. Dawson, "Age at Onset of Drug Use and Its Association with DSM," Results from the National Longitudinal Alcohol Epidemiologic Survey, *Journal of Substance Abuse*, reported in National Institute on Alcohol Abuse and Alcoholism (NIAAA), *Alcohol Alert: Underage Drinking,* 2006.
[16] National Center for Statistics and Analysis, *Fatalities and Alcohol Involvement Among Drivers and Motorcycle Operators in 2005,* August 2006.
[17] Levitt, S., Porter, J., Harvard University: National Science Foundation, 2002.

Chapter 8

Inhalants

> Inhalants are ordinary household products children use to get high. These products are found almost anywhere. Under a sink, in a desk drawer, a garage, storage shed... The products are inhaled by sniffing, huffing and bagging.

Did you ever play the "pass-out" game as a kid? I (Todd) remember playing with a few of my friends in junior high. We all stood in a circle. The object was for one person to take several deep breaths very quickly while a friend stood right behind him with his arms around the person's chest. Once the last breath was inhaled the friend would squeeze and hold his buddy's chest so tightly he couldn't exhale. The result usually meant getting light headed and feeling a little buzzed from the lack of oxygen to the brain. Sometimes it meant passing out completely for a second or two. From my adult vantage point, I wonder how kids think up such silly things.

Inhalants, like the pass-out game, work by removing the oxygen in the brain; but instead of the buzz lasting just until the next breath, inhalants have a much longer effect and can be fatal.

What are Inhalants?

Inhalants are not drugs. They are deadly vapors, fumes or gases that are intentionally inhaled in an effort to achieve a mind-altering experience. This can occur when a person ignores the warning labels of a wide variety of common household products. Some of these are the same products you so painstakingly worked to protect your children from when they first learned to crawl and walk. Products such as cleaning supplies, lighter fluid and gasoline were stored in cabinets under the sink with child-proof latches or on shelves in your garage more than three feet off the ground so your little one had no hopes of accidently ingesting said products.

Although many years may have passed and your child is well beyond the toddler stage, the poisonous products you once worried about are probably in the same place – in cabinets under the sink and on shelves three feet off the ground. But the concern and awareness you once had about those chemicals being *accidentally* ingested by a toddler should now focus on your pre-teen who might be tempted to *intentionally* inhale the dangerous fumes from those poisonous chemicals!

There are so many common household products that can be used as inhalants that locking them up, banning them from your house or preventing your child from obtaining them is virtually impossible. These products are found in every home across America. They're under sinks, in refrigerators, pantries, desk drawers, storage sheds and garages.

The best way to protect your child from using inhalants is educating him before he enters school. Unfortunately, when it comes to drug education, inhalants aren't often on a parent's radar screen; and some kids pay a price with their life.

It is easy to fall into the trap of saying, "My child would never do something so stupid." But consider that while only five percent of parents believe their teen has used inhalants to get high, almost 20 percent of 8th graders actually admit to using inhalants.[1]

> **Over one in seven 8th graders have used inhalants to get high.[2]**

Commonly Used Inhalants

Many products can be used as inhalants ranging from correction fluid to gasoline. And almost any product in an aerosol can

Inhalants

be used to get high: hair spray, air freshener, deodorizers, non-stick cooking sprays, computer air duster and spray paint (especially gold and silver, which have higher concentrations of the chemical toluene). Office and hobby supplies including felt-tipped markers, dry-erase markers, airplane glue and rubber cement can be used as inhalants. Cleaning agents and solvents such as spot removers and degreasers, nail polish remover, paint remover, lighter fluid and gasoline are also popular forms of inhalants. Kids even use whipped-cream dispensers to get high.

I (Todd) remember the very first traffic stop I experienced as a new police officer. I was still attending the police academy, and I was riding along with a veteran police officer on one of his shifts.

It was a dark night, and the flashing red and blue lights from the police car lit up the surrounding sky as we pulled over the car for a minor traffic violation, Sure enough, the car was loaded with kids who were out past curfew. While the officer lined them all up at the front of the car and began to write tickets for curfew violations, he asked me to look around inside their car for anything illegal. I thought to myself, "Wow, he is treating me just like his partner."

I jumped at the chance to do some real police work. When I returned to the police car after my search I proudly informed my "partner" that everything checked out okay. After a few phone calls to parents, the kids were released. It took me about twenty minutes to come down off the rush from that car stop. I thanked the officer for letting me help. I then told him when I was searching the car all I found was a balloon and a few socks rolled up like a donut on the floorboard. I confidently told him I was sure I would find a pellet gun because of all the CO_2 cartridges in the backseat; but after a thorough search, there was no gun to be found.

The officer looked at me for a long second; and then with a little condescending grin he told me what I saw in the car were items used as inhalants. What I thought were CO_2 cartridges were actually whipped-cream cartridges. The balloon was a whippet for catching and inhaling the propellant from the cartridges. The socks were rolled up to catch the whipped cream while the kids inhaled the propellant directly from the canister. I suddenly realized I still had a lot to learn!

Street Names for Inhalants

A few of the more common street names for inhalants are:
Bang
Boppers
Bullet
Climax
Head Cleaner
Huff
Kick
Locker Room
Moon Gas
Poor Man's Pot
Poppers
Rush
Snappers
Whippets (whipped cream cartridges)

A Short Spray Can Go a Long Way!

The sensation from getting high on inhalants is similar to getting drunk from alcohol. However, the rush from inhalants happens almost instantaneously and only lasts for about 30 to 60 seconds. However, the drunken-like effects can last for much longer.

Like drugs, inhalants can also be habit forming. What normally starts as a quick way to get high can lead to a long-time addiction. I once arrested a 30-year old man for shoplifting after he stole several tubes of airplane model glue. His need to get high was so bad he opened the tubes before he even got out of the store. It was sad and pathetic to see an adult covered from head to toe in airplane glue. He told me he started when he was a teenager and was never able to kick the habit.

How are Inhalants Used?

When a person uses inhalants, he breathes in the poisonous fumes through his mouth or nose. **Sniffing (or snorting)** refers to

Inhalants

breathing in the fumes through the nose, and **huffing** refers to using the mouth to inhale. There are a wide variety of techniques used in sniffing and huffing. Some users choose to sniff or huff the escaping vapors directly from the opened container. Some prefer to place a rag or sock soaked with the toxic solution directly over their mouth or nose while others will simply stuff the rag directly into their mouth. As if those methods aren't disgusting enough, others prefer to spray the chemical directly into their nose or mouth.

In an effort to be a little less conspicuous, some kids will paint their fingernails with a felt-tipped marker or correction fluid. They may also soak the cuff of their sleeve with paint remover or rubber cement during an art class and then enjoy themselves as they sniff and huff the rest of their school day away.

As a rookie officer I remember going to a disturbance call involving a juvenile party. Of course, police officers consider juvenile parties to be fairly routine occurrences. But when I entered the apartment, something was obviously different from anything I had seen before. There were about 25 kids crowded into a tiny, one-bedroom apartment, and none of them seemed to be fazed by a police officer standing in the room.

Many of them appeared to be drunk, but I didn't see any alcohol. I smelled a strong chemical odor that seemed familiar, but I couldn't place where I had smelled it before. When I walked into the bedroom I was shocked by what I saw. A 15-year-old boy was sitting on the floor holding a garbage bag over his head spraying gold paint into the bag. There were also several other garbage bags lying around the room with gold paint residue. The kids had been getting high by what's known as **bagging** paint!

It doesn't seem like it would take a rocket scientist to understand that breathing in toxic fumes and gases are dangerous, even deadly. After all, WARNING labels are on these products for a reason. But unless you have taken the time to teach your child the dangers of sniffing, huffing and bagging, he may think of it as a harmless way to get a buzz.

INVOLVED: Parents' Connection to Drug Prevention

How Kids Learn about Inhalants

The most common place for elementary-aged children to hear about sniffing inhalants is at school or on the school bus. But it's not just word of mouth. As mentioned earlier, today's young people are just one click away from complete details on **sniffing, huffing and bagging**. The Internet is full of "How To" instructions in chat rooms and on websites.

Things to Watch For

- Unusual odor coming from your child's mouth, clothes, room or other locations (basement, garage, etc.)
- Chapped lips or a rash around the mouth, lips and/or nose
- Fingernails painted with markers or correction fluid
- Paint on the lips, nose, face, hands and/or clothes
- Unexplainable items showing up in unusual places (i.e., a chemical-soaked rag stuffed behind boxes in the basement or airplane glue behind your child's bedroom drapes
- Missing items (i.e., nail polish remover, glue, hair spray) or a gradual disappearance of substances in containers you thought were full
- A drunken appearance that includes glassy eyes, slurred speech or stumbling while walking

The Parent Connection

Ideas to Help You Protect Your Child From Drugs

Talking about Inhalants

Because inhalants are cheap, legal and easily accessible to every child in any home, it's important to educate your children on the dangers of these toxic chemicals starting at an early age.

> **Tip # 8 on DRUG PREVENTION**
>
> Find Teachable Moments to
> Talk about Inhalants!

What to Say and What Not to Say

- Do explain to your child that inhalants are not drugs. They are poison.
- Do NOT explain the details of how inhalants are used. Your goal is to prevent your child from using inhalants, not provide step-by-step details on how to use them.
- Do explain the importance of having good ventilation when using chemicals such as gasoline, airplane glue and aerosol sprays to protect your brain, lungs and other vital organs.
- Do NOT let your child use toxic chemicals without adult supervision.
- Do explain inhalants are addictive.

TRY THIS IDEA!
Teach Your Children about the Dangers of Inhalants

1. Set a good example for children of all ages by letting them see you read and carefully follow the instructions on warning labels.

2. Teach your seven- to ten-year-old about inhalants with the following activity. Place a variety of common household products on the kitchen table. This might include a soft drink, non-stick cooking spray, salt, spray paint, mineral spirits and cooking oil. Ask your child to guess which products are poisonous and which are not. Then explain there is only one way to know if a product is poisonous, and that's by looking for a warning label. Ask her to search for the warning labels. When she finds one, have her read it out loud. Discuss the definition of words and phrases such as *fatal, toxic* and *adequate ventilation*. Make sure you explain these products are safe when used as directed. Then talk about the importance of breathing clean air to protect our brains, lungs and other vital organs. Continue to quiz your child over the next few weeks to reinforce what she learned in this activity.

3. During dinner or another time when you have a captive audience, explain to your children who are eight years old and above why you do not want them to ever consider using inhalants by sharing the following information.

When a person uses inhalants, he intentionally breathes in poisonous fumes, vapors or gases in an effort to get dizzy or high. However, because there is no way to measure the amount of chemicals being inhaled when one chooses to breath in toxic fumes, there is no way of knowing how much is too much until it's too late.

Sudden Sniffing Death Syndrome (SSDS) is the term used to describe when a person dies from using inhalants. In a matter

Inhalants

of one or two seconds, an otherwise healthy, bright young person can go from being dizzy – to passing out – to dying. This can occur the first, tenth or anytime inhalants are used.

Death from inhalants can occur in a variety of ways. For example, inhaling toxic chemicals causes dizziness; and it isn't unusual for the user to get so dizzy he actually passes out. There's also a good chance he'll become nauseated and vomit. Vomiting doesn't typically cause a person to die. But if he's unconscious when he vomits, he can die as a result of choking on his own vomit.

Inhalants also slow a person's breathing to such a low rate the person may stop breathing altogether and die. Inhalants can put so much stress on all the vital organs a young person can suddenly die from a massive heart attack. In other words…

> **A person using inhalants can go from dizzy to dead in a matter of seconds.**

HERE'S ANOTHER IDEA!
Incorporating Inhalants into Your Teachable Moments

When it comes to talking about inhalants, teachable moments can occur when you're cooking dinner, working in the yard or redecorating your child's room. For example, when the two of you are preparing a meal or baking cookies, mention that when you use non-stick cooking spray or other products in spray cans you only use them in a well-ventilated area.

Ask your child to read the warning label on the cooking spray and see if there is any mention about the dangers of inhaling the fumes. (NOTE: The back of the cooking spray in my kitchen states,

"WARNING...Use in adequate ventilation. Use only as directed. Intentional misuse by deliberately concentrating and inhaling the contents can be harmful or fatal.")

After your child reads the words from the can out loud, ask him what the word fatal means. Then you can say, "It's amazing some kids intentionally breathe in fumes from spray cans. But there is no way to know when you've breathed in too much until it's too late. That's why a person can go from dizzy to dead without any warning. That's why the manufacturer is saying that misuse can be *fatal*. But if you use it as directed – like we're doing in a large, open space in our kitchen – there's no danger."

Then look your child in the eye and say, "And if someone ever asks you or even dares you to breathe in the fumes from a spray can or gasoline or airplane glue, I want you to tell them, No! Let them know that using inhalants one time can kill a person, and you're not willing to risk dying to feel funny for a few seconds."

Another teachable moment can occur when you're doing home improvements. As you're painting the walls and baseboards in your house, use this opportunity to talk about the necessity of good *ventilation*. Ask your child to see if the manufacturer has a warning about ventilation on the paint can. After she reads the warning, ask her to open the windows so you don't get a headache, nauseated or dizzy from inhaling the *toxic fumes*.

When you're spray painting picture frames and shelves, ask your child to help you take the items to the backyard or driveway. On the way outside, talk about why the outdoors is better for tasks such as this. Not only is the clean-up easier, the open air prevents the concern of breathing in *poisonous* fumes.

When your child mows your yard or helps you with yard work, explain why it's important to open the garage door and move the mower to the driveway before filling the gas tank with gasoline. Not only does this help prevent any possible spills in the garage, it also provides the proper *ventilation* necessary for such a dangerous *toxic chemical*.

Inhalants

Reference

[1] The Partnership for a Drug-Free America, *Teens and Inhalant Abuse, 2006.*
[2] National Institute on Drug Abuse, *Monitoring the Future,* May 2008.

Chapter 9

Marijuana

> Marijuana is a mixture of dried, shredded leaves, stems, seeds and flowers of the cannabis (sativa or indica) plant. Most users smoke marijuana in a hand-rolled cigarette, a pipe or bong. Smoking a joint of marijuana provides an intoxicating euphoric high.

No other drug is likely to create more conversation today than marijuana! Simply ask someone in a crowded room what they think about the drug and soon a lively debate will begin.

Despite working as a narcotics detective and teaching narcotics classes for more than six years, I knew relatively little about marijuana's affects on society. I spoke very little about marijuana in my classes and I had very little opinion on the drug other than it was illegal and therefore people shouldn't be smoking or selling it. In some audiences, I would actually shy away from even bringing up the subject of marijuana because I was fearful I would offend someone who had used the drug. However, through extensive research, my knowledge and opinion about marijuana has dramatically changed.

It's important to pay close attention to this chapter. If your children are going to get involved in illicit drugs, this is the one they will most likely try first. **Marijuana is the most commonly used illegal drug in America.** More young people use marijuana than cocaine, heroin, ecstasy and the all other illegal drugs combined.

> **60 percent of kids who use illicit drugs use marijuana only.**[1]

According to most teens, marijuana is easier to purchase than alcohol. About 40 percent of teenagers say they could buy marijuana within a day and 20 percent indicated they could buy it within an hour.[2] The person supplying the drugs is typically a friend or acquaintance at school.

> **Almost half of high school seniors have used marijuana at least once in their lifetime.[3]**

Marijuana: What is it?

Marijuana is a psychoactive, mind-altering drug. It typically consists of a green/gray mixture of dried, shredded leaves, stems, seeds and flowers of the cannabis plant. The strength varies depending on where the plant was grown and which parts are used. For example, sinsemilla (which means without seed) contains only the buds of the female plant and is preferred by most users because of its added potency.

It's the delta-9-tetrahydrocannabinol or **THC** in marijuana that produces the mind altering effects. Over the past several decades the THC levels have continuously increased, making the marijuana of today far more potent than in years past. In the mid 1970s, the average THC content of marijuana was less than one percent. Today, the average THC is around 10 percent, but the more potent forms of marijuana can have levels higher than 30 percent.[4] Some marijuana proponents argue higher THC potency results in the user using less of the drug. Regardless of the amount one smokes, the end goal of the user is the same – to achieve a mind-altering and intoxicating high.

Street Names for Marijuana

There seems to be a never ending list of slang terms for marijuana, but some of the more popular ones are: pot, grass, weed, joint, reefer, hash, herb, skunk, getting wasted, Mary Jane, Texas Tea and Maui Wowie.

How Marijuana is Used

Marijuana is usually smoked in a hand-rolled cigarette called a **joint** or **nail**. There is approximately 0.4 grams of the plant material in each joint. Therefore, an ounce of *average* marijuana yields approximately 60 marijuana cigarettes. An ounce of marijuana containing higher THC levels requires less smoked plant material and can yield as many as 120 joints in a single ounce.[5]

Some users disguise their marijuana use by mixing the drug with the tobacco inside flavored cigars called **blunts.** The mixture also reportedly reduces the harsh effects of marijuana smoke on a user's throat. Others utilize a water pipe, commonly known as a **bong**, to buffer the marijuana smoke. Marijuana is also added to cookies, brownies or other food items and can be brewed into a tea. Marijuana is often used with alcohol, and occasionally mixed with cocaine or PCP for an added high.

When marijuana is smoked, the user inhales deeply and slowly. Then he holds it in his lungs as long as possible in an effort to absorb as much THC as possible. Within minutes the THC enters the brain and the intoxicating euphoric high kicks in lasting one to three hours. However, some of the adverse side effects of marijuana which can impair a person's ability to drive a vehicle may last up to 24 hours.[6]

Marijuana leaves many users feeling thirsty and hungry. Some will quench their thirst by drinking alcohol. Marijuana can also leave users feeling sleepy. For some, this is followed by a panic attack.

Marijuana is *NOT* Harmless!

In comparison to other drugs such as methamphetamine, heroin, or crack cocaine – marijuana may appear harmless. Don't be fooled! Remember, marijuana is the illicit drug your child is most likely to try at least once in his lifetime. Marijuana use, especially among youth, can have serious consequences. The earlier and/or the more often adolescents use marijuana the greater the risk for negative consequences. Marijuana use increases the risk of impaired mental health, delinquent acts, lower educational achievement, problematic use of other substances, sexual encounters and increased involvement in crime.[7]

Marijuana: The Gateway Drug

Some refer to the *marijuana gateway theory* as the *gateway myth*. The detractors point to the fact that the majority of marijuana users never progress to hard drugs. Therefore, they conclude there is no link between marijuana and the progression to other drugs.

It is true that most people who have tried marijuana do not go on to use other drugs. However, it is also true that marijuana users are far more likely to go on to use other illicit drugs *than non-users*. The Institute of Medicine stated: "Not surprisingly, most users of other illicit drugs have used marijuana first. In the sense that marijuana use typically precedes rather than follows initiation into the use of other illicit drugs, it is indeed a 'gateway' drug."[8]

According to the Center on Addiction and Substance Abuse, young people, 12- to 17-years-old, with no other problem behaviors who used marijuana at least once in the past 30 days are 26 times more likely to use another drug like cocaine, heroin, methamphetamine, LSD, or ecstasy than those teens who have never used marijuana (33.5 percent vs. 1.3 percent).[9] There may be several factors involved in the association between marijuana use and progression toward the use of other drugs. However, one of the best ways to prevent your children from using such drugs as cocaine, heroin and methamphetamine is to help them grasp the importance of *never* using marijuana.

> **62 percent of the adults who started using marijuana before age 15 eventually went on to use cocaine.**
>
> **Less than one percent of adults who never tried marijuana went on to use cocaine.**[10]

Marijuana and Addiction

Contrary to popular belief, some marijuana users do experience physiological and psychological dependence to the drug. Nearly one in ten users (9 percent) who have tried marijuana at least once will likely become dependent on the drug and one-third of daily users are at risk of developing a dependence on marijuana.[11]

A group of researchers found that 96 percent of chronic marijuana users who *voluntarily sought treatment* failed attempts to quit or cut down on their marijuana use. Ninety-five percent continued using marijuana despite persistent or recurrent psychological or physical problems. More than 83 percent reported they spent large amounts of their time buying, using, or recovering from the effects of marijuana. And 78 percent reported withdrawal symptoms.[12]

Numerous studies strongly suggest that marijuana withdrawal syndrome is a very real condition and the symptoms include significant increases in craving for marijuana, decreased appetite, sleep difficulty, anger, depressed mood, headaches, irritability, nervousness, restlessness and strange dreams.[13]

Unfortunately, many teenagers have bought into the lie that marijuana is harmless. For most, their first experience with marijuana often occurs with no apparent negative consequences. But for those who continue to use the drug, the desire to get high can become all consuming.

> **More American teenagers go into treatment for marijuana dependence each year than for alcohol and all other illegal drugs combined.**[14]

Charlie (name changed) was just ten years old when my wife and I moved into the house across the street from where he lived. Our families quickly became close friends and often shared holidays together. I remember vividly the photograph taken that first Thanksgiving. I had to work that day, but I came home during my break to enjoy some turkey and all the fixin's. Charlie was excited at the chance to see my police car and take a picture with me in my uniform. As I was walking out the door to go back to work, Charlie gave me a big hug. I can still remember his sweet and innocent smile.

Four years later I answered my front door to find Charlie's mom crying. In one hand was a small bag of marijuana she had found in Charlie's pocket. In the other hand was a homemade bong Charlie had pulled out of his closet after she confronted him. Charlie assured her he had only smoked marijuana a few times and promised it would never happen again. But over the next four years Charlie struggled to keep that promise. His parents turned to a reputable counselor in an effort to help Charlie stay clean and to cope with their own sorrow and concern over his drug use.

Things began to improve. Charlie graduated from high school, had a decent job and was about to enter college. And then . . . he smashed his car into a block wall after getting high and drinking a few beers. Luckily, Charlie was alone in the car and he wasn't injured. Charlie's mom was crying when she called to tell me about the accident and that her son had been taken to jail. Like every mother, she was worried about what it must be like for a young man to spend the night in a cold jail cell with other criminals. I knew he would be safe overnight in the county jail, but I went down to visit him.

Charlie was despondent as he walked in to the private meeting room. When he looked up and saw me sitting in the room, his eyes swelled with tears and the expression on his face was filled with shame and sadness. It was hard for both of us to talk for a few moments. I reassured him of his mother's love and promised we would all be there to help him get through this. As he was leaving the room to go back to the holding cell, I gave Charlie a big hug. We both wept. I can still remember seeing the brokenness in his eyes as he walked away.

I wish I could say Charlie has been drug free since that night, but that's not the case. While he's definitely made progress, there have been disappointing setbacks. Charlie and his family would be quick to say, "M*arijuana is not a harmless drug.*"

Marijuana and Health

Besides the THC in smoked marijuana, there are over 400 additional chemicals. The effects of many of these chemicals are still unknown, but some may result in serious health problems. Within the first few minutes of ingesting marijuana the heart rate increases significantly and so does the risk of a heart attack in some users.

Marijuana also decreases pulmonary function and may increase the risk of some cancers. Marijuana users are more prone to bronchitis and pneumonia than non-users.[15] Furthermore, studies suggest marijuana smoke contains 50 to 70 percent more carcinogenic hydrocarbons than tobacco smoke.[16] As a result, a person who smokes five joints a week may be taking in as many cancer-causing chemicals as a person who smokes a full pack of cigarettes a day.[17] In addition, a marijuana joint deposits three to four times more tar in the lungs than one filtered cigarette.[18]

Smoking marijuana may also be a major factor in the development of bladder cancer.[19] And although a recent study failed to find a positive association between marijuana and lung cancer,[20] the lead researcher commented that the study was important but not conclusive when he stated, "The fact that we didn't find, or failed to find an association [between marijuana and lung cancer] doesn't mean there isn't one."[21]

Marijuana on the Brain

Scientific studies have clearly indicated marijuana produces a negative impact on the brain. Young people who use marijuana have lower academic achievement than those who don't use the drug. Even short-term marijuana use has been linked to memory loss and difficulty with problem solving. Students who have a D or F average are more than four times likely to have used marijuana in the past year than students with an A average.[22]

But the risks of marijuana go beyond poor grades and forgetting a few things. Marijuana users are four times more likely to suffer from depressive symptoms including increased suicidal thoughts.[23]

Perhaps the most life-threatening effect of marijuana use is what it can do to a person's brain when he tries to operate a car. A moderate dose of marijuana can impair driving performance.[24] Marijuana is the second only to alcohol in substances found in drivers

INVOLVED: Parents' Connection to Drug Prevention

involved in traffic arrests and fatal car crashes.[25] Therefore, a young man who is typically capable of quick decisions when driving a car can find his perception off as he misjudges the speed of the on-coming traffic and proceeds into a busy intersection. Nearly 600,000 of the more than 4 million high school seniors in the United States admitted they drove under the influence of marijuana.[26]

Despite marijuana being the most widely used illicit drug, there is still much that is not known about its affects on the body. Today there are as many as fifty ongoing scientific studies in this area. According to Dr. Nora Volkow, director or the National Institute on Drug Abuse, "The most important thing right now is to understand the vulnerabilities of young, developing brains to these increased concentrations of cannabis (marijuana)."[27]

Watching for Signs

As a parent, you might notice your child's grades have dropped a little. Excuses are made. "The teacher doesn't like me." "The teacher's a moron and has no clue how to teach a class." Then, as time goes by, your child may begin to lose interest in sports, music or whatever was once her favorite past time. As you watch her grades continue to drop, you notice she's acquired a new group of friends. Her taste in clothes, make-up and music are changing – and not for the better! When you try to talk to her about your concerns, she gets annoyed and assures you she's fine. You desperately want to believe her, but you have your doubts.

Investigating a reported runaway is not typically the job of a narcotics detective, unless that person is suspected of staying at the house where there is an alleged methamphetamine lab and a federal fugitive from justice.

I went to the missing teenage girl's home and met her father. His daughter had been a runaway for nearly two weeks. He invited me into his home where he began to share details of the situation. He said his daughter had never run away in the past. She was a very good student and had never been in trouble at school or with the law. Prior to her running away, he noticed subtle changes in his daughter's attitude around the house as her grades began to slip. She was also

Marijuana

hanging out with a new girlfriend from school. But, it wasn't until his daughter ran away that he learned from several of her friends that the new friend was known to use drugs. He also learned this girl's father was rumored to be cooking and selling methamphetamine.

The father granted me permission to look around his daughter's bedroom. I was looking for drugs or drug paraphernalia. The first thing I noticed as I walked into the room was how well organized and clean it was. The bed was made with a bright multi-colored bed spread and her pillows were neatly arranged across the top of the mattress. Photos of friends were displayed on her desk. The clothes in the closet were all hung in an orderly fashion. As I looked around the room, I saw nothing that led me to believe this man's daughter might be using drugs. But, as I began to walk from the room I caught a glimpse in the mirror of a poster hanging on the back of her bedroom door. I closed the door to view the entire poster. I asked the father how long the poster had been on her door. He said about six months. Ironically, this was about the same time he began to notice the changes in his daughter. Curious, I asked the father if he knew what the poster was a depiction of and he replied he didn't. I explained to him the 20x40 poster was a very large psychedelic marijuana leaf.

In law enforcement we would call that poster a *CLUE!* However, this father knew little about marijuana. Although most parents can spot a marijuana leaf when they see one, every generation has new drug terms and associated paraphernalia to fill another book.

Maybe you have seen the number **420** written on a teen's notebook or somewhere in a public place. Do you know what that means to today's kids? 420 is used to acknowledge a time for smoking marijuana; and April 20th (4/20) has become something of a national holiday for marijuana users to celebrate use of the drug.

As a parent, warning signs might come in the way of changes in a child's behavior, declining school grades, new friends, or simple words or phrases written on their school notebook. It is important to continually learn about the ever changing drug culture and a little research through a search engine on the Internet can help you keep in touch.

Another term we have in law enforcement is *JDLR* or "just doesn't look right." If something with your child is JDLR, it is important for you to find out why and what is going on. The health, safety and future of your son or daughter might rely on it!

Maybe you are still wondering what ever happened to the runaway girl. Her father called me to say she returned home after seeing some things in her girlfriend's house that scared her. As for the fugitive, he was located after a little surveillance and turned over to the U.S. Marshall's Service.

The following are things that could serve as warning signs of marijuana use:

Side Effects of Marijuana

- Memory loss
- Difficulty in learning and concentration
- Impaired judgment and reaction time
- Loss of coordination and balance
- Panic attacks
- Paranoia
- Withdrawal from others
- Fatigue
- Dehydration
- Weight gain or weight loss
- Blood shot eyes / dilated pupils
- Coughing
- Chronic bronchitis
- Respiratory infections
- Increased heart rate
- Weakened immune system
- Anger and aggression
- Cancer of the head, neck and lungs

Marijuana

What to Watch For

- A small plastic bag of dried leaves
- Small hand-rolled cigarettes or rolling papers
- Greenish film on the tongue
- Dry cotton mouth
- Blood shot eyes and the use of eye drops
- Large dilated pupils in normal room light
  (Marijuana can also cause the pupils to pulse like a beating heart.)
- Skipping school
- A sweet burning odor of marijuana smoke
- Incense and deodorizers to cover the smell of marijuana
- Clothing, posters, or paraphernalia associated with drugs

Marijuana as Medicine

As previously stated, marijuana contains the chemical compound delta-9 THC which is classified as a cannabinoid. Marijuana also contains more than 60 other cannabinoids of which little is known about their effects. In the United States the Food and Drug Administration (FDA) has approved two prescription medications containing synthesized cannabinoid compounds and a third is undergoing clinical trials.

Marinol® and Cesamet®, two medications available by prescription, contain synthetic THC and may be safely prescribed and administered by physicians. These medications are used in treating cancer patients who suffer with nausea and vomiting following chemotherapy treatments and to stimulate the appetite of AIDS patients who need to gain weight. The FDA is currently conducting clinical trials for Sativex®, a mouth spray that contains pure THC extract which might provide relief of symptoms related to Multiple Sclerosis and neuropathic pain. The drug is already approved and being distributed by pharmacies in Canada.

For nearly 100 years, medications in the United States have been required to meet safety and efficacy standards and be approved by the FDA. These standards began to be challenged in the 1990s when voters in several states were asked to decide whether or not smoked marijuana should be used as a medicine.

In 1996, California's Proposition 215 and Arizona's Proposition 200 were the first voter ballot initiatives that passed in the United States allowing marijuana use for medical purposes. As of this writing, fourteen states have enacted laws which sanction the use of smoked marijuana as medicine: Alaska, Arizona, California, Colorado, Hawaii, Maine, Maryland, Montana, Nevada, New Mexico, Oregon, Rhode Island, Vermont, and Washington. Nearly all of these initiatives have been orchestrated by a marijuana lobbyist organization in Washington D.C. that supports the complete legalization of marijuana. Wealthy individuals, including financier George Soros, Peter B. Lewis of Progressive Insurance Companies, and John Sperling, founder of the University of Phoenix, have provided significant funding to promote passage of the initiatives.[28]

The Institute of Medicine concluded in its report, *Marijuana and Medicine,* that cannabinoids show promise for therapeutic relief of some illnesses and conditions. The American College of Physicians, The American Medical Association, American Cancer Society, and the American Academy of Pediatrics all support further research into the use of cannabinoids for certain medical conditions. Whether or not marijuana cigarettes are medicine is a determination best made by scientists through research, testing and the FDA approval process not by a majority of voters at the ballot box.

What the Experts Say

"Claims have been advanced asserting smoked marijuana has a value in treating various medical conditions. Some have argued that herbal marijuana is a safe and effective medication and that it should be made available to people who suffer from a number of ailments upon a doctor's recommendation, even though it is not an approved drug... [There] is currently sound evidence that smoked marijuana is harmful... no sound scientific studies [have] supported medical use of marijuana for treatment in the United States, and no animal or human

Marijuana

data supported the safety or efficacy of marijuana for general medical use. There are alternative FDA-approved medications in existence for treatment of many of the proposed uses of smoked marijuana."

U.S. Food and Drug Administration[29]

"Although marijuana smoke delivers THC and other cannabinoids to the body, it also delivers harmful substances, including most of those found in tobacco smoke... the report concludes that the future of cannabinoid drugs lies not in smoked marijuana but in chemically defined drugs."

Institute of Medicine[30]

"...AMA recommends that marijuana should be retained in Schedule I of the Controlled Substances Act...," meaning it has no acceptable medical use and high potential for abuse. "...AMA believes that the National Institutes of Health should use its resources and influence to support the development of a smoke-free inhaled delivery system for marijuana or delta-9-tetrahydrocannabinol (THC) to reduce the health hazards associated with the combustion and inhalation of marijuana..."

American Medical Association[31]

"No scientific evidence has been found that demonstrates increased benefits and/or diminished risks of marijuana use to treat glaucoma compared with the wide variety of pharmaceutical agents now available."

The American Academy of Ophthalmology[32]

"Studies completed thus far have not provided convincing evidence that marijuana or its derivatives provide substantiated benefits for symptoms of Multiple Sclerosis."

National Multiple Sclerosis Society[33]

Despite these statements, more states are presented with voter initiatives or legislative amendments to allow marijuana to be used as medicine each year. In support of their cause, proponents often cite that marijuana provides relief to the sick that no other prescription drug offers. Steve Kubby, a longtime marijuana user and co-founder of

Prop. 215, recently stated "I learned that Marinol is an acceptable, if not ideal, substitute for whole cannabis [marijuana] in treating my otherwise fatal disease…this discovery was a fantastic turn of events for me, because guaranteeing a stable supply of pot is expensive and dangerous."[34]

Cannabinoids may have potential for the treatment of some medical conditions, and research should continue in this area. Approving medicine by voter popularity, however, is a dangerous precedent. Enacting state laws that allow for the use of marijuana as a medicine circumvents the FDA drug approval and safety processes, violates federal laws, and fosters an unregulated system of distribution that is open to abuses and criminal enterprises.

Rev. Scott Imler, another Co-Founder of California's Prop. 215 stated "We created Prop. 215 so that patients would not have to deal with black market profiteers. But today it is all about the money. Most of the dispensaries operating in California are little more than dope dealers with store fronts."[35]

What Parents Need to Know

- Teens caught with marijuana can be slapped with a large fine and/or sent to jail. If a person is caught a second time, or if he is caught selling the drug, the punishment is more severe.

- Marijuana can show up in the urine on a drug test anywhere from a few days up to a few weeks after using the substance.

The Parent Connection

Ideas to Help You Protect Your Child From Drugs

Dealing with Your Own Past

Many parents avoid discussing drugs with their children because of their own previous drug use. A past history of smoking pot, drinking alcohol or snorting cocaine seems to leave many parents feeling stripped of their right to approach this subject. Parents often say they feel it would be hypocritical to tell their child not to do drugs since they themselves were known to sneak out and get stoned when they were younger. Obviously these parents don't understand the meaning of the word hypocrite. A parent who tells their child to avoid drugs and then turns around and gets high on pot is a hypocrite, not a parent who did drugs 10 or 20 years ago and now understands the dangers of drug use.

If you stop and think about it, there are probably a number of things you tell your child not to do even though you did them when you were a child. For example, you probably played in the street when you were kid, but that didn't stop you from telling your child not to play in the street when he first ventured in the front yard. You've probably said a hundred times, "No snacks before dinner." Yet how many times have you eaten a snack before dinner? By the way, did you ever cheat on a test, lie to your parents or steal some candy when you were young? Has that ever prevented you from teaching your children it's wrong to cheat, lie or steal? It shouldn't, because instilling strong values is all a part of good parenting no matter what you did or didn't do as a child. Remember, this isn't about your past. It's about your child's future.

So this brings us to the next tip in the Parent Connection to Drug Prevention.

INVOLVED: Parents' Connection to Drug Prevention

> **Tip #9 on DRUG PREVENTION**
>
> Be Prepared To Answer The Question –
> "So Mom, Dad, Did You Ever Use Drugs?"

What to Say about Your Past

If you're one of those fortunate people who escaped the drug scene when you were growing up, this is a no-brainer! When your child asks if you did drugs, you can proudly hold your head up and say, "No, I didn't." But don't stop there. Go ahead and explain why you didn't use drugs and how you managed to successfully avoid them. Talk about any difficult situations you encountered because of your stand on drugs. Discuss how others treated you when they learned you didn't use drugs. Did they respect you or treat you with disdain? If you were made fun of, explain how you handled the peer pressure and how glad you are you held true to your convictions. Tell your child about friends who used drugs and any problems they may have encountered as a result of their choices.

If, on the other hand, you did use drugs, you can simply say something like the following:

You know, I did experiment with drugs when I was growing up. But back then there was little drug prevention going on, and I didn't know much about the dangers of drugs. You and I are fortunate because today we know how dangerous drugs are. Therefore, it's very important to me that you protect your future, your body and your brain by taking a strong stand against drugs.

That's it! That's all you need to say. If your child starts pumping you for more information, you can simply say, "I'm not proud of what I did, and I really don't want to dwell on this."

Your child doesn't need to know the details of your drug experiences. There's no need to explain what it felt like to get high or which drugs you used. If, on the other hand, you think it could help your child to understand the price you paid for your drug use, such as poor grades, memory loss, an automobile accident, etc., then go ahead and share more details about the negative consequences. Just don't glamorize the actual experience of using drugs.

Your honesty may actually strengthen your relationship with your child. Most young people would prefer to have real parents – not so-called "perfect" parents. A mom and dad who admit their mistakes and talk openly about the consequences of their actions without glorifying those actions may actually help keep their child on a positive track.

Building Trust

A common complaint of today's young people is the lack of trust their parents have in them. Yet it's impossible to trust a child who sneaks out of the house, steals money out of Mom's purse or skips school.

As a result, your children need to understand trust is earned – not given. And while it takes years to build trust, it can be destroyed by one quick, misguided decision. Then the rebuilding process starts over again.

As a parent, it is your responsibility to set an example for your children. If you want them to be honest, respectful and kind to others then you must constantly model those character traits. When you slip up and fail in one of these areas, you need to continue to set the example by admitting you were wrong and asking for your child's forgiveness. This will help your child learn to admit her mistakes and not cover them up.

> **If you want me to trust you, you must be trustworthy.**

INVOLVED: Parents' Connection to Drug Prevention

HERE'S A GREAT IDEA!
Declaration of Honesty Policy

Talk to your children about how honesty builds trust. Let them know that as you gain confidence in their ability to be totally honest with you, you will then be more comfortable giving them freedom to make their own choices, go more places and do more things. But remind them that when they aren't honest, the reverse will also be true.

Discuss how communication builds trust. Let your child know you expect to hear about unusual situations from him and not from others. Give him examples of actions that can jeopardize your ability to trust him. For example:

- You find out from your neighbor that drugs were used at the party your child attended Friday night.

- You find out from a friend that your child was called to the principal's office for disrupting class.

- You find out your child went to an R-rated movie instead of the PG-13 movie you had agreed upon.

After this discussion, set an "Honesty Policy" for your home. Inform your children you will strive to be honest and never lie to them, and you expect them to do the same. This means you will be honest in all areas of your life, including where you are going, who you will be with and when you will be home. Let your children know you expect them to do the same.

HERE'S ANOTHER HELPFUL SUGGESTION!
Eight Reasons to Say No to Marijuana

Make sure your child understands where you stand on the use of marijuana by sharing the following information. (Note: Don't be afraid

Marijuana

to be fanatical on this issue. According to a national study, children who think their parents would "somewhat" disapprove of them trying marijuana once or twice were over five times more likely to have used marijuana in the past month than the kids who said their parents would "strongly" disapprove of them using the drug.[36]) So be bold and tell your child under no circumstance is she ever to use marijuana. Remind her she has an awesome brain, a bright future; and you don't want her brain or future to go up in smoke!

1. Some people say marijuana is harmless, but that is not true.
2. Marijuana is an illegal drug. Teens caught with marijuana can incur a large fine and/or go to jail.
3. Within the first few minutes of ingesting marijuana, the heart rate increases significantly and so does the risk of a heart attack in some users.
4. A marijuana joint deposits three to four times more tar in the lungs than one filtered cigarette.
5. Marijuana use can produce memory loss. Young people who use marijuana typically achieve less academically than those who don't use marijuana.
6. Marijuana is second only to alcohol in substances found in victims of fatal automobile crashes. It only takes a moderate dose of marijuana in the past 24 hours to impair a driver's ability to make quick decisions.
7. More American teenagers go into treatment for marijuana dependence each year than for alcohol and all other illegal drugs combined.
8. It is rare to find a person addicted to cocaine or heroin who didn't begin his drug use with marijuana. One of the best ways to prevent an addiction to cocaine and heroin is to avoid using marijuana.

TRY THESE IDEAS!

Beware of the Boring Summer Months!

Many teens turn to marijuana simply because they are bored, and teens are bored more in the summer months than at any other time of the year. Over 6,300 young people experiment with marijuana for the first time each day in June and July, 40 percent more per day than during the rest of the year.[37]

Make sure your child is well supervised and too busy to get bored during the summer months. Some ideas to consider are:

- Have a list of chores for your child to work on each day.
- Provide fun projects for your child to work on during the summer (i.e., redecorate their bedroom, paint, make curtains and matching bedspread, etc.)
- Require your child to read a book every week during the summer.
- Take a family vacation.
- Enroll your child in a class at a nearby community center or college.
- Spend time with your child swimming, playing tennis, flying kites, going on picnics and volunteering in your community.
- If your child is old enough, require him or her to get a part-time job such as babysitting, mowing yards, lifeguarding, working as a clerk at a store or in an office. (Make sure part of that money goes to a worthy cause such as saving for college, a car, or camp. Too much extra, readily available spending money can also lead to drug use.)

Suspecting Drug Use

One Friday night a senior in high school came home reeking of an unusual odor. The mother immediately suspected marijuana. When she confronted her son, he admitted he had indeed used marijuana that evening as well as on two other occasions in the past few weeks. The mother was extremely disappointed in her son's decision since she had diligently communicated over the years about the dangers of drugs.

She spent the weekend talking with close friends and relatives about reputable child psychologists and counselors. First thing Monday morning she made an appointment for her son to meet with a counselor. While some may see this as overreacting, this mother knew it was important her son understand his decision to use drugs was not acceptable. She also knew he was leaving for college in six months, and she wanted to try to get to the root of the problem before he left home.

If you suspect your child is using drugs, whether it's inhalants, alcohol, marijuana or cocaine, confront him. If he admits to using drugs, seek professional help. The risks associated with drug use are huge and can last a lifetime. A simple slap on the wrist and warning may have no impact whatsoever.

If he denies using drugs, don't dismiss your suspicions. Obviously, something about your child's behavior or actions has gotten your attention. Stay alert. Keep a watchful eye on your child's emotions, attitude, friends and activities. If something still seems off kilter and your child won't communicate about what's going on in his life, seek professional help. Your child needs to know you will go to any extreme to protect him from drug addiction. He also needs to understand you will never consider the use of drugs as a whimsical phase that will pass.

In seeking help, make sure you turn to someone who is reputable and has experience in working with teens and dealing with risky behaviors. It's also important to make sure the professional shares your family values regarding teen involvement in alcohol, drugs and sex. If you don't know a person to turn to, ask your physician, school principal and/or clergy for suggestions.

INVOLVED: Parents' Connection to Drug Prevention

References

[1] Parents the Anti-Drug, *Marijuana Facts: Myths and Facts About Marijuana,* www.theantidrug.com/EI/myths-and-facts-about-marijuana.asp

[2] The National Center on Addiction and Substance Abuse (CASA), *Teen Survey: High Stress Frequent Boredom, Too Much Spending Money: Triple Threat That Hikes Risk Of Teen Substance Abuse, 2003.*

[3] National Institute on Drug Abuse, *Monitoring the Future – National Results on Adolescent Drug Use Overview of Key Findings 2007*, May 2008.

[4] Marijuana Potency Monitoring Project in 2007, University of Mississippi, June 2008. www.cnn.com/2008/HEALTH/06/12/pot.potency.ap/

[5] Dale Gieringer, Ph.D., *Economics of Cannabis Legalization*, Quick American Archives, Reprinted from Ed Rosenthal, ed., Hemp Today, 1994, pp. 311-24.

[6] The National Center on Addiction and Substance Abuse (CASA), *Non-Medical Marijuana: Rite of Passage or Russian Roulette?* April 2004.

[7] Robert Roffman, ed., James Berghuis, et al.,) "The Teen Cannabis Check-Up:Exploring Strategies for Reaching Young Cannabis Users," *Cannabis Dependence: Its Nature, Consequences, and Treatment*, Cambridge University Press, 2006, p. 276.

[8] Janet E. Joy, et al., Institute of Medicine, "First do No Harm: Consequences of Marijuana Use and Abuse," *Marijuana and Medicine: Assessing the Science Base,* National Academy Press, 1999, pp. *99-100.*

[9] The National Center on Addiction and Substance Abuse (CASA), *Non-Medical Marijuana*, April 2004.

[10] Joseph C. Gfroerer, et al., *Initiation of Marijuana Use: Trends, Patterns and Implications,* Substance Abuse and Mental Health Services Administration (SAMHSA), Office of Applied Studies, 2002, p.71.

[11] Thomas F. Babor, "The Diagnosis of Cannabis Dependence" in Robert Λ. Roffman and Robert S. Stephens, ed., *Cannabis Dependence, Its Nature, Consequences, and Treatment*, Cambridge University Press, 2006, p. 31.

[12] Ibid. p. 29.

[13] Aron H. Lichtman and Billy R. Martin, "Pharmacology and Physiology of Cannabis Dependence" in Robert A. Roffman and Robert S. Stephens, ed., *Cannabis Dependence, Its Nature, Consequences, and Treatment*, Cambridge University Press, 2006, p. 50.

[14] Substance Abuse and Mental Health Services Administration (SAMHSA), "Admissions Aged 12-17 by Primary Substance of Abuse: TEDS 1992-2000,"*Treatment Episode Data Set (TEDS), Table 5.1a*, April 1, 2002.

[15] D.P. Tashkin, "Pulmonary Complications of Smoked Substance Abuse." *West J. Med*, 1990, 152:525-530, also "What Americans Need to Know About Marijuana," ONDCP www.whitehousedrugpolicy.org

[16] D. Hoffman, K.D. Brunnemann, G. B. Gori, and E.E.L. Wynder. "On the Carcinogenicity of Marijuana Smoke," in V.C. Runeckles, ed., *Recent Advances in Phytochemistry*, New York: Plenum, 1975. See also NIDA, "Research Report Series: Marijuana Abuse," Oct. 2002, www.nida.nih.gov/ResearchReports/Marijuana/Marijuana3.html)

[17] National Institute on Drug Abuse, "Marijuana: Facts Parents Need to Know," 2007, www.nida.nih.gov/marijbroch/parentpg13-14N.html

[18] T.C. Wu, et al., "Pulmonary Hazards of Smoking Marijuana as Compared with Tobacco," *New England Journal of Medicine, 1988,* 318:347-351.

[19] The Library of Cancer, "Pot Smoking Could Raise Odds for Bladder Cancer" found at www.yourcancertoday.com/Cancers/Urinary-Cancer/Risk-Factors/Articles/Pot-Smoking-Could-Raise-Odds-for-Bladder-Cancer/23/2/8888/searchSort=-3&searchPage=2&searchQ

[20] Dr. Donald Tashkin, UCLA Geffen School of Medicine, "*Marijuana does not Raise Lung Cancer Risk*, www.foxnews.com/story/0,2933,196678,00.html
[21] "All Clear:: An interview with Dr. Donald Tashkin" *High Times*, August 17, 2006. www.hightimes.com/news/mikeg_ht/3658
[22] National Household Survey on Drug Abuse, "The NHSDA Report: Marijuana Use among Youths," 2002.
[23] Gregory B. Bovasso, Ph.D., "Cannabis Abuse as a Risk Factor for Depressive Symptoms," *American Journal of Psychiatry, 2001; 158:2033–2037*.
[24] National Institute on Drug Abuse, "Marijuana Abuse," *Research Report*, June, 2005, The National Highway Traffic Safety Administration..
[25] National Highway Traffic Safety Administration (NHTSA) Notes. Marijuana and alcohol combined severely impede driving performance. *Annals of Emergency Medicine* 35(4):398-399, 2000 and Non-Medical Marijuana III: Rite of Passage or Russian Roulette? A CASA White Paper, June 2008.
[26] U.S. Office of National Drug Control Policy (ONDCP) "Marijuana Fact Sheet," 2005.
[27] Benedict Carey, "Marijuana Use is Pushing Teens into Treatment," *Los Angeles Times,* April 26, 2004, www.drugstory.org/feature/LATimesArticle.asp
[28] Gary Goldberg, "Wealthy Ally for Dissident in the Drug War," *New York Times,* September 11, 1996. query.nytimes.com/gst/fullpage.html?res=9BOCE7DF1E32A2575ACOA 960958260&s&spon=&pagewanted=all
[29] U.S. Food and Drug Administration (FDA). "Inter-Agency Advisory Regarding Claims that Smoked Marijuana is a Medicine," April 20, 2006, www.fda.gov/bbs/topics/NEWS/2006/NEW01362.html
[30] Janet E. Joy, et al., Institute of Medicine (IOM), *Marijuana and Medicine: Assessing the Science Base,* 1999.
[31] American Medical Association, *Policy Statement H-95.952*, June 2001. www.ama-assn.org/meetings/public/annual01/csa_reports.pdf
[32] American Academy of Ophthalmology, *Complimentary Therapy Assessment: Marijuana in the Treatment of Glaucoma,* May 2003.
[33] National Multiple Sclerosis Society, *National MS Society Information Sourcebook: Marijuana,* 2006.
[34] CA Norml News, "Steve Kubby Released After Serving 62 Days In Jail", April 14, 2006 www.canorml.org/news/kubbyarrested.htm
[35] Office of National Drug Control Policy, *Medical Marijuana Reality Check*, February 2007.
[36] The National Household Survey on Drug Abuse, *The NHSDA Report, Parental Disapproval of Youths' Substance Use,"* August 2002. *Findings from the 2002 National Survey on Drug Use and Health,* 2003.
[37] Substance Abuse and Mental Health Services Administration (SAMHSA), "For Many Youth, Summer Means First-Time Substance Use," *SAMHSA News,* 2004.

Chapter 10

Prescription Drugs

> The prescription and over-the counter drugs found in most medicine cabinets are the very pills today's teens are using to get high. In fact, these medications are now more popular among teens than all the other illicit drugs, with the exception of marijuana.

Imagine the following scene: a beautiful field of flowers gently swaying in the breeze as soft, soothing music plays in the background. An attractive young couple sees each other across the field and run toward one another, ending in a loving embrace.

This scene is taken directly from a television commercial promoting a pharmaceutical drug marketed for social anxiety disorder. But the love affair portrayed in this commercial shrinks to insignificance when compared to the love affair going on between the pharmaceutical companies and television and radio advertising.

In 1997, the Food and Drug Administration (FDA) opened the door for pharmaceutical companies to begin Direct-to-Consumer (DTC) advertising through radio and television commercials. Since that time, the pharmaceutical companies' love affair with television and radio has blossomed. Billions (yes, with a B) have been spent on advertising pharmaceutical products through the use of print, radio and, of course, those often eye-catching television commercials.

The pharmaceutical industry spent $985 million on DTC advertising in 1996. By 2005, annual DTC advertising increased 330 percent to more than $4.2 billion dollars.[1] During the same period pharmaceutical companies also increased promotional spending on their products in other areas such as professional promotions for doctors and free samples,

DTC advertising is an effective marketing tool and provides potential benefits by opening the door for informed conversations between patients and their doctors. However, one researcher stated that to an unprecedented degree, DTC pharmaceutical advertisements portray "the educational message of a pill for every ill – and increasingly an ill for every pill."[2] As we have seen with marketing for fast food, children's toys and many other commercial products, advertising has a powerful way of affecting the attitudes and norms of Americans, especially our vulnerable children.

Introducing Generation Rx

Today's teens are less likely to use illegal drugs such as cocaine, ecstasy, heroin and meth than previous generations. Yet they are increasingly more likely to turn to the family medicine cabinet or walk to the corner drugstore for their next high.

Drug dealers, track lines, needles and pipes are being replaced with prescription and over-the-counter (OTC) drugs. Teenagers who have a desire to get high know pain relievers, tranquillizers, sedatives, stimulants and cough suppressants can send them flying high. The use of prescription and OTC drugs by today's teens has been so dramatic that some have labeled them **Generation Rx.**

- Nearly one in five teens has abused a prescription medication to get high.
- One in 10 teens has abused OTC products such as cough medicine to get high.
- Two in five teens believe prescription medications, even when not prescribed by a doctor, are much safer to use than illegal drugs.

- Nearly one in three teens believes there's nothing wrong with using prescription medicines without a prescription once in a while.[3]

Want to Pop a Pill?

So where are all these prescription drugs coming from? Most teen users of prescription pills say they get their prescription and OTC drugs from their friends and family. Opening Mom's and Dad's medicine cabinet can provide an almost continuous supply of Vicodin®, OxyContin® or other painkillers. Some teens say it's easier to get OC (OxyContin®) than marijuana.

> **More than three in five teens say prescription pain relievers are easy to get from their home medicine cabinets.[4]**

But it's not just home medicine cabinets that are being raided. There's the vast array of medicine cabinets that can be pilfered while babysitting, visiting relatives or watching TV at a neighbor's house. A clever teen may excuse himself and go to the bathroom. While there, he fumbles through a medicine cabinet, taking one or two pills from this bottle and a couple from that bottle; and in most cases, no one will be the wiser. Then it's off to the Saturday night "Pharming-Party." No, this isn't a party held in the middle of a cornfield. This term refers to parties where teens trade prescription drugs.

The pills are often dumped in a big bowl or plastic bag. Then the wide array of pills, including pain relievers, anti-depressants, sedatives and stimulants in various colors, shapes, and doses, are passed around the room. **Trail Mix is the term used to describe this wide variety of pills.**

Some teens carefully eye each pill before making their selection as if it were a delectable box of chocolates they were about to consume. Others haphazardly grab several pills and chase them down with a beer, wine cooler or whatever happens to be the available beverage of choice for the evening. Then they wait with great anticipation to see just how high their selected assortment of pills might take them.

Abusing Prescription Drugs

The most commonly abused prescription drugs include:

- Opioids – used to treat pain.
- Central Nervous System (CNS) Depressants – used to combat anxiety and sleep disorders.
- Stimulants – used to treat Attention Deficit/Hyperactivity Disorder (ADHD) and Narcolepsy.

Unfortunately, many of today's youth believe because these drugs are prescribed by a doctor, they must be safe and less addictive than illegal drugs. In fact, **more than one quarter of today's teens believe prescription painkillers are not addictive**.[5] But they're wrong. There's actually little difference between the effects of some prescription drugs, such as OxyContin®, when they are misused and illegal drugs such as Heroin.

Mixing Drugs

One of the many problems associated with abusing prescription drugs is they are not a one-size-fits-all. Before prescribing any medication, a doctor always asks pertinent questions such as: What allergic reactions have you experienced in the past? What other medicines (prescription and non-prescription drugs) are you taking? What is your general health? What is your age, height and weight? Then the appropriate medication and dose will be prescribed.

But, when a teen chooses to self-medicate and haphazardly takes different medications, there can easily be a duplication of chemicals; or the drugs may interact with each other in adverse ways. Mixing drugs has been a problem among the elderly for years as they take the prescription drugs prescribed by their doctors and then self-medicate themselves with a wide variety of OTC and mail-order drugs. Taking a combination of medications without knowing how they react with each other is extremely dangerous. This is true whether the person is a senior citizen, a teenager or anyone in between. Yet the number of teenagers who are popping prescription drugs for recreational purposes is staggering.

- One in five teens has abused Vicodin® - Painkiller
- One in 10 teens has abused OxyContin® - Painkiller
- One in 10 teens has abused Ritalin® and/or Adderall® - Stimulant [6]

Prescription Pain Relievers

Opioids, also known as narcotic analgesics, are commonly prescribed to relieve moderate to severe pain typically resulting from cancer, surgery or injuries. Morphine and Codeine are two narcotics prescribed by doctors to relieve pain. Trade names for other pain relievers include OxyContin®, Percodan®, Percocet®, Vicodin®, Lorcet®, Lortab®, Darvon®, Demerol® and Lomotil®.

Ironically, the medications often considered miracle drugs by those living with chronic pain are the same drugs some teens are using to get bombed on Saturday night. When taken under the supervision of a doctor, there is little chance of serious side effects or addiction. But those who don't follow their doctor's orders and exceed the recommended dosage or use opioids for recreational purposes can find themselves in serious trouble.

Those abusing pain relieving drugs frequently develop a **tolerance** resulting in a need for stronger doses. Increased dosages can lead the user down the path of **addiction.** Overcoming an addiction to prescription pain medication can be difficult and painful. The abuser often finds he is no longer taking stronger doses for the euphoric high, but he's taking the pills to simply cope with the pain of the **withdrawal symptoms.** Some describe the pain of withdrawal as ten times worse than having the flu. By this point, it may be difficult to continue with everyday life as the addict becomes consumed with his need for more drugs. Those desiring to kick the habit often have no option but to enter rehab. And some are never able to kick the habit despite the large amounts of money spent or the number of months or years spent in rehab. At this point, addiction becomes a way of life – a living nightmare that won't go away.

The pain of being addicted, especially to OxyContin®, leads some to violent crime in order to support their habit. There are reports all around the country where desperate addicts commit robberies of elderly patients and pharmacies to obtain the drug.

Symptoms of Prescription Drug Abuse

- Irritability
- Hot/cold flashes
- Runny nose
- Uncontrollable coughing
- Chronic joint and bone pain
- Muscle spasms
- Involuntary leg movements
- Uncontrollable body shaking
- Abdominal cramping
- Vomiting and diarrhea
- Heart palpitations
- Paranoia
- Depression

Street Names for Prescription Pain Relievers

OxyContin:
  Oxy, Oxycotton, Oxy 80s, Hillbilly Heroin, Poor Man's Heroin

Vicodin:
  Vike

Hydrocodone/Acetaminophen:
  Watson-387

Prescription Sedatives and Tranquilizers

The medical term for prescription sedatives is Barbiturates, and the term for prescription tranquilizers is Benzodiazepines. Both types of drugs are considered Central Nervous System (CNS) depressants. They are used to reduce tension, anxiety, panic attacks and sleep disorders by slowing normal brain activity. When taken as prescribed, they can provide a calming effect and greatly improve a person's quality of life. Commonly abused CNS depressants are Librium®, Valium® and Xanax® – all frequently found in the family medicine cabinet.

These drugs are typically monitored carefully by a doctor and prescribed for short-term use because **tolerance, addiction and withdrawal symptoms** can occur quickly. Then the abuser finds himself dealing with a new set of problems including insomnia, mood changes, phobias, depression and suicidal thoughts.

It's also important this type of drug never be increased beyond the prescribed dosage without a doctor's approval, and it should never be stopped abruptly. Otherwise, painful withdrawal symptoms may occur. And since stimulants and tranquilizers often result in drowsiness, they should *NEVER* be mixed with alcohol or other medications that might provide a sedating effect. This combination could dramatically slow the breathing process, as well as the heart and respiration rate, to a point which can be fatal; and there's the primary problem.

Teens who use drugs for recreational purposes aren't interested in following guidelines for a recommended dose; nor do they consider the dangers of combining various drugs or washing them down with alcohol. Too often teens who mix drugs are looking to experiment with the combinations for new experiences. Some users blend doses of drugs to prevent hard crashes when coming down off their high. Sedatives such as Xanax® are sometimes combined with stimulants for this reason. (Remember, a teen is operating from the *Emotion Center* of the brain, not the *Wisdom Center*!)

Symptoms of Sedative and Tranquilizer Abuse
- Irritability
- Slurred speech

- Disorientation
- Lack of coordination
- Memory loss
- Shallow breathing
- Impaired judgment
- Paranoia
- Aggression

Street Names for Sedatives and Tranquilizers

Candy, Downers, Sleeping pills, Tranks, Z-bars, Bars

Stimulants

Stimulants such as Ritalin®, Adderall® and Dexedrine® are a few of the drugs prescribed for Attention Deficit Disorder (ADD), Attention Deficit Hyperactivity Disorder (ADHD), Narcolepsy and short-term treatment for obesity. These drugs stimulate the central nervous system and enhance brain activity causing increased alertness, attention and energy. When taken as directed by a physician, stimulants have been proven to be safe, effective and are not addictive.

However, some young people have learned prescription stimulants can also provide an amazing high. Others may turn to the drugs to pull an all-nighter to cram for finals. And if losing weight is a concern, stimulants can help by suppressing a person's appetite.

To experience a quick and more intense high, the user crushes several tablets together and either snorts the powder like cocaine or injects it like heroin. Stimulant abuse can provide distinct dose-dependent plateaus ranging from mild visual perceptions to a complete out-of-body experience. But after a while, the euphoric highs tend to be replaced with feelings of hostility and paranoia as the user unknowingly becomes addicted. As with most drugs, once addicted, larger doses are needed as the user unsuccessfully strives to regain the original experience. At this point, blood pressure, heart rate, temperature and respiration may begin rising to dangerous levels. For some, this can result in a fatal seizure or heart attack.

Interestingly, those abusing drugs such as Ritalin® and Adderall® often obtain their supply from friends at school who legitimately obtain these prescription drugs for medical purposes. Those young people probably don't realize the harm in allowing a classmate to use their medicine to get a little high. Some students who are legitimately prescribed the drugs make a little money selling their prescriptions but more than likely don't consider themselves drug dealers. A colleague once investigated a mother who sold her son's medications. This unscrupulous mother went "doctor shopping" and had her son's prescription filled by two doctors. She gave one prescription to her son for his medical needs, and she sold the other.

Symptoms of Stimulant Abuse

- Headaches
- Fatigue
- Insomnia
- Enlarged pupils
- Confusion
- Nervousness
- Irritability
- Loss of appetite
- Dizziness
- Skin rash and itching
- Abdominal pain
- Vomiting
- Severe depression
- Paranoia
- Hallucinations
- Sensation of creatures crawling under the skin
- Delusions
- Increased body temperature
- Increased heart rate and blood pressure

INVOLVED: Parents' Connection to Drug Prevention

Street Names for Stimulants

Kibbles and Bits, Kiddy Cocaine, Pineapple, Rids, Skippy, Smarties, Smart Drug, Uppers, Vitamin R, West Coast

Other Prescription Drugs

Unfortunately, today's youth experiment with many prescription drugs to boost the high from one drug and minimize the crash from another or simply experiment with a mixture looking for the ultimate high. A few other drugs being abused today include, Wellbutrin®, Zyban®, Zoloft®, Prozac®, and Paxil®.

Over-The-Counter Drugs (OTC)

Have you ever found yourself standing in the drugstore staring at the wide array of remedies for colds and coughs? The choices are overwhelming – especially if you haven't mastered commonly used terms such as decongestant, suppressant, expectorant and antihistamine. Even after you make the decision of which drug to buy, you then have to choose between tablets, capsules, gel caps, syrups and lozenges.

While this may be terribly confusing for adults, there are many teenagers who know more about these medications than their own parents. In fact, some teens are so experienced at **robotripping** and **robodosing** they've become **syrup heads**.

Now if that statement made absolutely no sense to you, don't feel alone. Most parents aren't aware that the current trend among an alarming number of teens is to get high by guzzling large doses of Nyquil®, Robotussin® or other similar cough syrups. Thus the terms – robotripping, robodosing and syrup heads.

Cough suppressants aren't the only OTC medications kids are abusing today. They also abuse motion-sickness pills, diet pills and sleep aids. But Dextromethorphan, (pronounced: dextro-meth-or-phan), or easier yet, **DXM**, is by far the most coveted ingredient when it comes to OTC recreational drug use. A recent government study found that 3.1 million people between the ages of 12 and 25 have used OTC cough-and-cold medicine to get high. The same study reported females between the ages of 12 and 17 were more likely than males to have misused OTC medications containing DXM whereas males were more likely than females in the 18-25 age group.[7]

DXM is an ingredient found in over 140 products on the shelves in your local supermarket or drugstore. It's most often found in cough suppressants including Robotussin®, Nyquil®, Vick's Formula 44® and Coricidin HBP Cough and Cold Medicine®. As a result of increased abuse, several states and local jurisdictions have passed laws to limit access to all OTC medications containing DXM. Customers must ask for and sign for the drugs at their local pharmacy, and in some locations, proof of age is required. (Perhaps you have a bottle of one or more of these in your medicine cabinet.)

When used as directed, OTC medications containing DXM are safe and effective. But, as already stated, teens who use these drugs aren't concerned about "using as directed." Plain and simple, they want to get high! It may take 10 times or more the recommended dose to get the desired high from cough medicine. The effects can last up to 8 hours and range from a simple buzz to an out-of-body experience similar to tripping on PCP or LSD.

I *(Todd)* first learned of DXM nearly ten years ago while I served a search warrant related to a narcotics investigation. The drug dealer was selling several types of illegal drugs, but he found that selling pure DXM was particularly lucrative. Twelve kilos (roughly 25 pounds) of the substance was seized from a shipment from China via Canada.

The drug dealer kept records and emails detailing his numerous illegal narcotics transactions. As I searched through these, one in particular jumped out at me. The correspondence was sent to the drug dealer from one of his customers warning him that he should be more careful regarding how he conducted his business. The email went on to explain that recently a sister of one of his customers had contacted him, also via email, questioning the identity of the DXM drug dealer. Her brother had died from a DXM overdose, and she wanted to find the man she believed was responsible for selling him the substance. The same email had a forwarded copy from the deceased man written shortly before his death. It read: "What is this world coming to when

INVOLVED: Parents' Connection to Drug Prevention

your drug dealer shows up for a delivery with his eight-year-old daughter in the car?"

I was able to learn the identity of the young man, and I contacted his father on the telephone to learn more about his son. He told me Mike had learned how to use DXM to get high from the Internet at 16. He had his first overdose at 17, and he was dead shortly after his 18th birthday. Mike was his only son. Unfortunately, I could not officially link the drug dealer to the young man's death.

Symptoms of OTC Drug Abuse

- Confusion
- Impaired judgment
- Blurred vision
- Dizziness
- Paranoia
- Excessive sweating
- Slurred speech
- Nausea and vomiting
- Abdominal pain
- Irregular heartbeat
- High blood pressure
- Headache
- Lethargy
- Numbness of fingers and toes
- Redness of face
- Dry and itchy skin
- Loss of consciousness
- Seizures

Street Names for OTC Drugs

Candy, CCC, Dex, DM, DRX, Red Devils, Robo, Rojo, Skittles, Triple C, Tussin, Velvet, Vitamin D

Warning Signs of Prescription or OTC Drug Use

- Medicine mysteriously disappearing
- Unfamiliar pills in your child's belongings
- Unfamiliar prescription drug bottles or bottles with the label removed in your child's belongings
- Continuous need for cough medicine
- Slurred speech
- Staggering
- Sweating
- Dry mouth
- Blurred vision
- Dilated pupils
- Numbness in fingers and toes
- Red face
- Hallucination

The Going Price

Besides the fact that prescription and OTC drugs are legal and FDA approved, they're also extremely cheap. If a teen is unable to steal the desired pill to get high, he can always purchase a few pills for next to nothing. Prices vary, depending on location, but typically the going price for Ritalin® is a dollar or two per pill. Vicodin® sells for about $5 a pill. OxyContin® is stronger and, therefore, more expensive. It usually sells for about $1 per milligram. Thus a 10-milligram tablet sells for about $10.

The Parent Connection
Ideas to Help You Protect Your Child from Drugs

What's a Parent to Do?

The same medications doctors prescribe to improve a person's health and quality of life are increasingly being abused to enhance the supposed pleasures of life. What does it matter if the recommended dose is increased, mixed with other drugs and chased down with alcohol? Who cares if the pills are crushed and snorted or injected? These drugs are both legal and FDA approved. In the mind of a teen looking for a good time – they must be safe!

This is the mindset your children may have unless you are *involved* in ongoing, heart-to-heart talks discussing the dangers of using prescription and OTC drugs outside of their intended dosage and recommended use. It's important to share the dangers of abusing all types of drugs – illegal, prescription and OTC drugs. And don't beat around the bush. Make sure your child knows exactly where you stand.

With a Click of a Mouse . . .

Besides acquiring pills from a medicine cabinet, today's teens can also go on line to replenish their stash. **Internet pharmacies**, occasionally referred to as **Pill Mills,** put prescription drugs at the fingertips of anyone, any age and sometimes with no prescriptions needed. That means with a click of a mouse and a credit card your child can place an order for his favorite prescription drug. The most common prescription drugs offered through Internet pharmacies are Xanax®, Valium®, Vicodin® and OxyContin®. These are also among the most abused prescription drugs.

Prescription Drugs

This is one more reason why parents need to carefully monitor children's Internet use and credit card purchases. If you don't know how to monitor the Internet, learn how!

This brings us to the next step in the Parent Connection to Drug Prevention.

> **Tip #10 on DRUG PREVENTION is**
> Regularly Monitor Your Child's Computer

Other Points of Interest on the Internet

The Internet also provides kids with a never-ending supply of information regarding drugs. For example, simply by surfing the Web, your child can obtain detailed instructions on how to achieve the various plateaus of DXM found in cough medicine. If he wants to learn how to avoid the common problem of nausea that often accompanies extremely large doses of cough syrup, the web provides simple, step-by-step instructions on refining the cough medicine to obtain an almost pure form of DXM. Or, with the click of the mouse and a credit card, a kid can have pure DXM tablets shipped directly to his home. Since many young people come home to an empty house after school, intercepting a delivery before a parent arrives home from work is no problem.

Seek and Ye Shall Find

Take a few minutes to browse the Internet. You might be amazed at what you can learn about drugs. For example, just by using the search engine, you (or your child) can easily find:

- Chat rooms and blogs to learn how to use drugs and evade law enforcement
- How to pass a drug test
- Drug terminology and slang terms

INVOLVED: Parents' Connection to Drug Prevention

- A do-it-yourself recipe for methamphetamine and other synthetic drugs
- How to purchase marijuana seeds and grow your own crop
- How to make crack cocaine
- Instructions on how to roll a marijuana joint
- How to purchase drug paraphernalia, including those disguised to look like everyday household products such as Magic Markers, lighters, lipstick cases, etc.
- Helpful hints on how to enhance your experience when using drugs
- Where to find drugs
- The going price for drugs
- The location of Raves (parties using ecstasy and other club drugs.)

HERE'S AN IDEA!

Beware of the Location of Your Computer

Four simple rules make it difficult for anyone to abuse the privilege of surfing the web.

- Do not allow your child to have Internet access in his bedroom.
- Keep the computer with Internet access in a high-traffic area such as the family room or kitchen.
- Make sure the computer is turned so all who walk past can easily see the computer screen.
- Install Internet-protection software that screens and limits access to certain web pages on all computers.

HERE'S A FEW MORE IDEAS!

Four Things Your Child Needs to Know about PRESCRIPTION AND OTC DRUGS

Make sure your child knows that:

1. Just because prescription drugs are legal and approved by the FDA does not mean they are safe when used outside a doctor's recommendation.
2. Prescription drugs should never be used without the supervision of a doctor.
3. Combining certain prescription or OTC drugs with alcohol can result in death.
4. If prescription or OTC drugs are abused, they can lead to an addiction and a long list of serious problems including heart attack and death.

Don't Take Chances

Now that you have finished this chapter, make sure you check your medicine cabinets and dispose of all unused medications. If you have current prescriptions, make sure you put them in a secure location. Your concern shouldn't be limited to your own child, but also your child's friends who may frequent your home. Then there are your nieces and nephews, the babysitter, cleaning lady, exterminator, plumber and anyone else who might have access to your house. The risk of someone abusing your medications is too great! To put a little spin on a popular credit card company's slogan, "What's in your cabinet?"

References

[1] J. Donohue, M. Cevasco, M. Rosenthal, "A Decade of Direct-to-Consumer Advertising of Prescription Drugs," *The New England Journal of Medicine,* August 16, 2007.

[2] B. Mintzes, *"*For and Against: Direct to Consumer Advertising is Medicalising Normal Human Experience," *British Medical Journal,* 2002;324:908-911 www.bmj.com/cgi/content/full/324/7342/908

[3] Partnership for a Drug-Free America, *Key Findings on Teen Drug Trends (PAT 2005)*, "Generation Rx: A Culture of Pharming Takes Root," May 2006.

[4] Ibid.

[5] Ibid.

[6] Ibid.

[7] Substance Abuse and Mental Health Services Administration, *New Study Reveals More Than 3 Million Adolescents and Young Adults Have Used Non-Prescription Cough and Cold Medicines to Get High at Least Once in Their Lifetimes,* January 10, 2008.

Chapter 11

Ecstasy
(MDMA)

> Ecstasy is a synthetic drug that acts as a stimulant and hallucinogen causing something like a psychedelic effect on the user. Simply put, when a person uses this drug, he has an abundance of energy; and his perception of life and the world around him changes.

What if someone handed your child a small pill and said: "Swallow this and you'll have self-confidence and more energy than you could ever imagine. This pill will make you feel total acceptance and love by all those around you. You'll feel a peace like you've never experienced in your life. And ... there are no dangerous side effects."

Do you think your child would swallow the pill? Thousands of young people across America do every day. And they find out that almost all the hype about this little pill is true. Word has it ecstasy produces a high beyond words. It provides a chemically induced happiness resulting in enough energy to allow a person to party tirelessly all through the night. What is this magical pill? It's . . .

methylenedioxymethamphetamine

Okay, if that's too big of a word to pronounce, just remember MDMA. Better yet, try the more common name – ecstasy.

Street Names for Ecstasy: E, X, XTC, Roll, Hug Drug, Love Drug, Adam, Bean, and Essence.

> **If you want to know if someone is high on ecstasy just ask, "Are you rolling?"**

The Streets of Vegas

To most it seemed like any other day in Las Vegas. Airplanes lined up over the horizon bringing visitors from around the world to the Las Vegas strip. This two-mile stretch of road is lined with mega-resorts that play host to more than 30 million visitors each year. It's the only place on earth where one can walk from the Statue of Liberty to the Eiffel Tower, stand before the Sphinx or ride a gondola through Venetian canals all before noon. However, to Jim, Elsa and a small gathering of family and friends this is not any other day. It is the 22nd birthday of their daughter Danielle.

We sit in their modest home just outside the neon lights of Las Vegas where Danielle grew up. The coffee table displays her pictures, and I (Todd) look through the photos as they silently tell me the story of her life. I am honored to be a guest in Danielle's home for the celebration of her birth.

Her proud parents share stories of her growing-up years that make us laugh. Jim recalls his repeated checks on the small strawberry patch off the back porch. With each visit he was anxiously hopeful to reap the red, juicy rewards of his labor. But time and again he found only small green and pale-white strawberries. He finally came to the conclusion that birds were to blame for the absence of ripe, ready-to-eat fruit. But then early one morning he found five-year-old Danielle in the garden in pajamas and stocking feet. As she turned toward the house, her eyes met Jim's, and the sticky-sweet smile on her young, innocent face finally revealed the truth. Some in the room have heard the story before. This time, however, the tale carries a deeper meaning for everyone.

A year earlier I was working as an undercover narcotics detective in Las Vegas. My partners and I started handling cases involving a drug we knew very little about. On the street, they called it ecstasy.

Ecstasy (MDMA)

Most of the drug cases we conducted involved dimly lit transactions in seedy alleyways or abandoned parking lots, but ecstasy cases were different. To locate this drug we had to venture under the brightly lit marquis of hotel casinos into the crowded and often lavish nightclubs. Inside the clubs' doors we found an environment none of us had seen before.

It had been nearly twenty years since disco-tech revolutionized a generation, and now "techno-music" was breathing life into the dying dance clubs. The techno clubs offered more than just music. This is where ecstasy made a resounding debut.

At an independent mega-club located in a 5-star hotel resort and casino, the drug flowed freely; and everyone knew if you wanted ecstasy, this was the place to find it. Despite the years of experience as police officers in "Sin City," we were all shocked on the first night of our investigation into the drug activity there. Hundreds of club-goers were in drug-induced trances, hypnotized by the fast-paced music. Drug dealers boldly approached interested buyers. In just a few hours, we witnessed four victims of drug overdoses wheeled from the club by paramedics. We made three more visits to the club and decided the activity at this four-story drug den was larger than we could quell. I met with vice-presidents of the hotel-casino on July 19th to advise them of our findings and to ask for their intervention. At the conclusion of the meeting I stated, "If something isn't done, it is just a matter of time before someone dies."

A birthday celebration brought Danielle and her friends to this club that very night. Looking for the ultimate high, the group turned to ecstasy. Danielle began to feel sick early on. She could hardly stand. Her head was pounding while her stomach churned. Her friends were baffled. This had never happened before. Surely, they thought, something else was to blame. Danielle was driven to a nearby house that she had never been to before. She lay on the bed as the others went back to the party. When her friends returned, they found her dead. Danielle spent the last agonizing hours of her life in a strange room with no one by her side. She died less than 24 hours after I spoke those unfortunate, prophetic words to the hotel-casino vice-presidents.

I never met Danielle. Had it not been for that fateful night, I may never have known her name. Her closest friends later revealed she had only taken ecstasy three times, and the third time it killed her.

INVOLVED: Parents' Connection to Drug Prevention

According to the coroner's report, the only drug in her system was ecstasy. Danielle's tragedy has been told repeatedly across the country through public service announcements distributed by the Partnership for a Drug Free America. Her father's emotional declaration at the conclusion of a 30-second spot will echo in my soul for a lifetime, "A parent is not supposed to outlive their child. It's not the scheme of things."

> **A parent is not supposed to outlive their child.**

What Ecstasy Looks Like

Ecstasy typically comes in brightly colored pills with a myriad of pictures embossed on the pills. It might be cute cartoon characters, a happy face, a dove or the letter E. Well-known logos such as the Mitsubishi star and Nike's "swoosh" emblem are also popular emblems on ecstasy. The little pills are often camouflaged on a candy necklace or in a Tic-Tac container.

How Ecstasy is Used

Ecstasy is most often used in pill form. It's also available as a powder or in crystal form. It can also be smoked or sniffed.

The History Behind Ecstasy

The drug was developed in 1913 by Merck, a German pharmaceutical company. It sat on the shelf for years with no real purpose. In the 1970's it gained some acceptance as a means to encourage psychotherapy patients to communicate their feelings.

By the 1980s, ecstasy found its destiny as a **club drug**. At the time, it was unregulated; but in 1985 it was put in the same category of other dangerous narcotics as heroin and cocaine. That means ecstasy is illegal to manufacture, sell, buy or consume. However, in the late

Ecstasy (MDMA)

1990's, ecstasy had become the club drug of choice and could be found in nightclubs and Raves across the country. A **Rave** is a party where young people dance nonstop to loud, pulsating, hypnotic techno-music. Young people across the country flock to Raves each weekend.

A Rave might take place in a private nightclub, warehouse or in an open field. These parties often continue all weekend. Raves are typically advertised as alcohol free. But don't be fooled. Many people who attend Rave parties use ecstasy and other drugs in order to endure the long hours of constant dancing.

Getting High on Ecstasy

Regular users of ecstasy are typically older teens and young adults in their early to mid-twenties. Although a single pill costs less than a dime to manufacture, it typically sells for $20 to $45 on the street.

It takes about 30 minutes for ecstasy to kick in, and the high lasts four to six hours. Since the drug enhances sensory perception, loud, pounding, percussion music actually makes the user feel good. A person using ecstasy who is normally known as a quiet introvert will suddenly find himself sharing intimate thoughts and feelings with anyone willing to listen. Those high on ecstasy are overcome with warm, loving, accepting feelings and crave to be touched by others – thus the name love drug.

Those using ecstasy are often seen staring transfixed at glow sticks or glowing jewelry. Others might put mentholated rub in and around their nose while wearing surgical masks to increase the effects of the high.

Ecstasy users are often seen sucking on a pacifier or candy sucker. This isn't because they're reverting back to their childhood. It's because ecstasy causes muscles to tense and teeth to grind.

What Goes Up Must Come Down

While young people often say there are no negative side effects to ecstasy, it isn't true. A common problem associated with this drug is what's known as the **comedown**. While ecstasy provides a euphoric high on Friday and Saturday nights, the user often experiences something known as the ecstasy blues by the time he returns to work or school on Monday morning. The euphoric weekend is over, and the user is left feeling irritable and depressed, longing for the next high.

The Addictive Power of Ecstasy

Ecstasy does not cause a physical addiction like cocaine or heroin or the nicotine craving smokers experience with cigarettes. But, many use the drug compulsively because they are psychologically addicted to the drug-induced high. Using ecstasy on a regular basis can quickly result in a **tolerance** to the drug requiring larger doses to reach an acceptable high. It is with great disappointment that most users find it impossible to duplicate their first euphoric high.

What's in a Pill?

Chemically speaking, ecstasy is closely related to amphetamines and hallucinogens. Pure ecstasy is not common. So what is in any given pill is anyone's guess.

When I (Todd) was working undercover, it was common to purchase counterfeit pills being sold as ecstasy. The counterfeit pills would sometimes be nothing more than starch and fillers. However, on many occasions, the pills contained another drug or a combination of drugs. Sometimes the effects were similar to ecstasy; other times the effects were extremely different. In any case, the user could potentially suffer from severe reactions from the counterfeit pills.

Several groups began testing the pills at raves and other venues. The test is capable of identifying only one drug – ecstasy. Even if the screening test identifies ecstasy, that doesn't mean it isn't laced with another drug such as ephedrine, Ketamine or LSD. The screening test also fails to provide the amount of ecstasy in a pill. Therefore, street testing for illegal drugs provides a false sense of security. But the truth is, ALL illegal drugs carry certain dangers associated with their use.

Ecstasy and Memory Loss

Research now indicates that using ecstasy can produce both long-term and short-term memory loss after a single use. In an analysis of 26 studies involving 600 users, researchers from Hertfordshire University in England found that 75 percent of the users had a significantly impaired memory compared to those who have never used ecstasy. Lead researcher, Dr. Keith Laws stated, "Often when you ask people who take ecstasy if they have memory problems, they say no, but when you test them, they realize they have serious problems."[1]

Other Concerns

Perhaps the greatest concern of ecstasy use is its ability to control the body's temperature control system. As the body reaches dangerously high temperatures, the user sweats profusely and will quickly dehydrate. High temperatures can lead to renal failure.

This is why those high on ecstasy consume large quantities of water. But drinking too much water can affect the balance of electrolytes. Both extremes of dehydration and drinking too much water can result in death. Note: In a six-year time span, ecstasy-related emergency room visits in the U.S. increased from 253 to 4,026.[2]

Ecstasy and the Law

Ecstasy is an illegal drug. Help your children understand that just as with other illegal drugs, if they give ecstasy away, sell it or use it, they could end up being charged with a fine, a prison sentence and a criminal record!

Side effects to Ecstasy:
- Personality change
- Mood swings
- Anxiety
- Depression
- Panic attacks

INVOLVED: Parents' Connection to Drug Prevention

- Appetite change
- Dehydration
- Nausea
- Insomnia
- Dilated pupils / blurred vision
- Difficulty concentrating
- Confusion
- Memory loss
- Tremors / Muscle tension
- Clenching of teeth
- Increased body temperature and blood pressure
- Chills and/or sweating
- Seizures and strokes
- Kidney, liver and cardiovascular failure
- Increased risk of HIV and other STDs

Drug paraphernalia used with Ecstasy:
- Pacifiers
- Suckers
- Lots of water
- Glow sticks or glowing jewelry
- Surgical-type masks & mentholated rub
- Loud, pulsating, hypnotic, techno-music
- Candy necklaces
- Tic-Tac containers
- Straws

What Parents Need to Know

1. Ecstasy can remain positive in a drug test as long as one to two weeks after use.
2. Ecstasy is often hidden or camouflaged in Tic-Tac containers, candy wrappers, candy necklaces and straws.

Ecstasy (MDMA)

The Parent Connection

Ideas to Help You Protect Your Child From Drugs

Be There for Your Child

Parents of toddlers are constantly on the lookout for ways to protect their child from household dangers. There are plastic plugs that insert into electrical sockets, child-proof latches for the cabinets and even little gates to confine the child to a particular room or away from a staircase.

It's amazing what parents go through to protect our children in those early years, especially considering what an inconvenience all those gadgets can be to undo, step over and dig out. Despite all the frustrations though, wasn't it worth protecting your children and knowing you didn't have to worry about them poking a paperclip into an electrical socket or falling down the stairs? If your children have now reached school age, the good news is – the days of annoying protective gadgets are over. That phase of your life is in the past! But the days of physically being there for your children won't be over as long as they live under your roof.

Perhaps one of the most important things you can do as a parent to protect your teenage children from drugs, alcohol and sex is to be available for them when they come home in the evening. Think about it! Don't you think it would be far more difficult for a child to come home drunk or high on marijuana or ecstasy if he knew his parents were always waiting up for him when he got home?

So this brings us to the next tip in the Parent Connection to Drug Prevention.

Tip #11 on DRUG PREVENTION is

Wait Up for Your Child

INVOLVED: Parents' Connection to Drug Prevention

Wait Up? ... You've Got to be Kidding!

Oh, I can almost hear you moan. You may even be tempted to skip the next couple of pages at this very moment ... BUT DON'T! The information that follows may be the most important bit of advice this book has to offer. It may be the very thing that prevents your child from using drugs.

Okay, no one is going to suggest that waiting up for teenagers is fun. It certainly causes the frustration of installing electrical plug covers and childproof latches on cabinets to shrink to insignificance. But isn't protecting your teen from the dangers of drugs just as important as protecting the busy toddler from exploring under the kitchen sink? A teen who knows his parents will always be waiting up for him when he gets home at night will be far less likely to use drugs than a teen who knows his parents will be fast asleep when he gets home.

Think of a 16-year-old girl who's just started to date. The first few times she gets home she can hardly wait to share every last detail of the evening with her mom. A few weeks later she walks in the front door, shouts toward the family room, "I'm home. See you in the morning." She then goes directly to her bedroom and closes the door.

Her mother suddenly senses red flags! Why didn't her daughter want to talk tonight? Did something go wrong on the date? Is her daughter upset? Could she be hiding something? Maybe it's nothing. Maybe she's just tired. Or maybe it has something to do with alcohol, drugs or sex. A wise mother will go to her daughter's bedroom and ask her how her evening went, just to clear up her unanswered questions. But if mom is already in bed when her daughter comes home, mom will never see those red flags.

(*Marilyn*) If you've read any of my other books or if you've heard me speak at a conference, you know waiting up is one of the suggestions I *always* give parents. The reason I do this stems from my own experience as a teenager. In high school, I had an 11 o'clock curfew. Like clockwork, I walked in the front door every Friday and Saturday night at 11 o'clock. I was never late. As a result, I suppose my parents never saw the importance of waiting up.

Every Friday and Saturday night I walked in the front door, turned off the light and walked down a dark hallway to my bedroom.

Ecstasy (MDMA)

However, had my parents ever waited up, they would have been surprised at what they found. No, they wouldn't have smelled alcohol or become suspicious of drug use. But my appearance would have been a dead give-away. You see, I didn't look the same at 11 o'clock as I did when I left home earlier that evening. My hair was messed up, my clothes were wrinkled and my face was flushed. Had they waited up, they would have figured out what was going on.

The interesting thing is, if they had waited up for me on a regular basis, I'm confident the physical activity would have never even started in the first place. As I've already stated, I loved my parents; and I had a tremendous desire to please them. Therefore, I don't think there was any way I could have looked my mom and dad in the eyes after messing around on my dates with Chuck. But there was something about being able to go to my bedroom, shut the door and sleep for eight hours before I had to face them. I suppose this helped suppress my feelings of guilt.

After seeing the heartbreak etched in my parents' faces upon learning their youngest daughter was pregnant at the age of 17, there's no doubt in my mind they would have given anything to roll back the clock and wait up for me to return home. No doubt countless numbers of parents who have watched their children suffer through the horrors of drug addiction have wished the same thing. But it's so easy to convince yourself, "It won't happen to my child."

I also wonder how many parents go to bed before their children come home at night because subconsciously they don't want to know what their children are doing. It seems far easier to put their head on a pillow and hope for the best as they drift off to sleep rather than to deal with problems as they occur. These same parents might even find themselves questioning a recent change in their child's behavior and for a fleeting moment wonder, "Could this be the result of drugs?" but then quickly dismiss the thought as a phase that will soon pass.

A child who rolls his eyes in disgust and stomps out of a room is going through a phase. A teen who uses drugs and alcohol is not going through a phase. Drug use is a criminal offense and can lead to a life-long addiction that can absolutely destroy your family. It's important to understand that it is far easier for parents to deal with issues such as drugs, alcohol and sex in the early stages than trying to pick up the pieces after the fact. There is probably no better way to know if your child is involved with risky behaviors than to wait up and engage in a conversation when he or she walks in the door in the evening.

TRY THIS IDEA!

Wait Up and Smell the Aromas!

A young man once told me (Marilyn) there was no way he could drink, do drugs or even hang around kids who did these things because his mother always greeted him at the door each evening with a smile and a hug! He said he knew she would smell the aromas surrounding his evening the moment he walked in the door.

It's important to wait up for your child, not because you don't trust him, but because you love him. If you set a decent curfew, preferably no later than midnight for high school students, then this should not be difficult. The following are some suggestions that might make this more workable:

1. You and your spouse take turns waiting up so you only pull a shift every other time.

2. Watch a movie, read a book or play a computer game while you wait up.

3. If you can't stay awake, go to bed in your child's bed. That way you'll be forced to get up when he gets home.

4. If you just have to go to bed, set your alarm for 15 minutes before your child is due home. After the alarm goes off, wash your face and be prepared to greet your child with a friendly smile. (Note: Don't worry. There's no way your child will come home early and catch you sleeping. *Teens never come home early!*)

The point is – the best thing you can do is be alert and prepared to engage in a conversation when your children walk in the door. Some evenings the conversation may be no more than one or two minutes. Other nights it could go much longer. Either way, be there for your children just as you were always there when they were toddlers.

Waiting Up Demonstrates Love

A young lady once told me (Marilyn) she had a midnight curfew her senior year in high school. She said she always came home to find her father sitting in his chair awaiting her arrival. They would sit and talk for a few minutes, and then her dad went to bed, knowing his daughter had made it home safely; and she went to her room, reminded of her father's love.

After graduation, she enrolled in the local college. Her father told her he was removing her curfew. He did, however, explain he expected her to make good choices and be home at a reasonable hour. The first night she came home at one o'clock. Much to her surprise her father was sitting in his chair waiting for her. They did their usual brief discussion, but he made no comments about the late hour. The next week she was out until 1:30. When she got home, there was her dad waiting up for her. This time she sat down next to him and said, "Look, Dad, you said you were doing away with my curfew. So now that I'm staying out later, you don't need to be waiting up for me anymore. I know you have to go to work in the morning."

Her father gently smiled and simply said, "Well, you're the most precious thing in my life; and as long as you're living under my roof, I'll be waiting up for you no matter what time you get home."

She told me from that day on she never stayed out past midnight out of respect for her father. That was an impressive, responsible decision on her part! The years of her father waiting up for his daughter were not just about protecting her from drugs or at-risk behaviors, but they also gave her a strong sense of security, love and self-worth, a foundation that will empower her to make good choices that will lead to life-long success.

A Special Note to Dads

I *(Todd)* have been very candid in this book about the relationship I had with my father as well as the relationships I have with my sons. Fathers must wake-up and realize the important role they play in their children's lives. There are too many children growing up today with absent dads. Ironically, these absentee fathers are often living under the same roof with their children. That's not to say every man who has a successful career is a lousy father. There are some amazing dads who are successfully juggling a busy workload and heavy travel schedules while staying *involved* with their children. But all too often, success in the workplace interferes with the connection between parent and child.

Unfortunately, many dads today don't know how to be a good dad because they had no role model in their own lives. Some may have had a father who lived at home but was always too busy to attend a Little League game or school play. Maybe their dad was the strong, manly father who showed little affection and felt his job was simply to be the provider and disciplinarian. Or perhaps, like in my case, there was the father who wasn't around much at all for various reasons. It is often difficult for men to know how to be the right dad.

I challenge each father reading this book to give building relationships with your children as high a priority as providing food, clothes and shelter for them. If your present job doesn't allow quality time with your family, then perhaps you're in the wrong job.

As parents, we all have demands upon us; and we will all make mistakes in raising our children. But nothing is more significant to our children than our taking the time to show interest in them and their world. A simple hug, a "good job" or "thank you" and frequent "I love you" can make all the difference in the world. How do I know? Because I still feel the emptiness in my life from not having that from my dad. However, I have seen the impact those simple things have done for my sons' lives.

HERE'S ANOTHER HELPFUL SUGGESTION!

Share the Seven Reasons to Say NO to Ecstasy with Your Child

1. Ecstasy produces a euphoric high. But a person using ecstasy can build tolerance to the drug requiring larger doses to get the desired high.

2. Ecstasy Blues often occur after the high is over, leaving the person feeling irritable and depressed.
3. Ecstasy causes muscles to tense and teeth to grind.
4. Ecstasy can cause memory loss.
5. Overdosing on ecstasy can easily occur since the dose can vary greatly from pill to pill.
6. Ecstasy takes over the body's temperature control system. The user sweats profusely as the body reaches dangerously high temperatures. This can lead to kidney damage and renal failure.
7. Ecstasy is an illegal drug. If you give it away, sell it or use it, you could end up with a criminal record and find yourself behind bars.

References

[1] K. Laws, *"New Research Reveals the Effects of Ecstasy on Memory Function,"* School of Psychology University of Hertfordshire, Reuters Press Release – *Single Use of Ecstasy Causes Life-Long Damage,* June 26, 2007.

[2] Substance Abuse and Mental Health Services Administration (SAMHS), *Club Drugs: 2002 DAWN Update Highlights,* 2002.

Chapter 12

Cocaine

> Cocaine is a stimulant that enhances brain activity. It provides an almost immediate euphoric high, providing a sense of strength, energy and uninhibited sexual desires. Cocaine can cause a person to be talkative and mentally alert as it reduces the need for food and sleep.

If that were all your child knew about cocaine, he might be tempted to give it a try. That's why you need to be prepared to tell him the rest of the story.

What Cocaine Does

Cocaine is a powerful stimulant that is highly addictive. It produces an intense high within seconds, but the euphoric effects are short lived and followed by a crash that leaves the user in a deep state of depression. Desperate to feel better, the user goes back for another hit. He then experiences another momentary high followed by another round of depression.

It doesn't take many cycles of ups and downs before the user is addicted. In fact, **cocaine is so highly addictive it isn't unusual for a person to become hooked the very first time he tries the drug.** When he eventually hits bottom and decides to kick the habit, he slips into an even deeper depression followed by paranoia and anxiety attacks. Desperate to feel normal, he snorts, injects or smokes cocaine once again. But the controlling power of cocaine never makes him feel normal. It only destroys him.

INVOLVED: Parents' Connection to Drug Prevention

So the very drug that provided the amazing high and caused alertness and energy now sucks the very life out of him. Gone is his sharp memory and ability to concentrate. In other words, the positive effects that lure a person into using cocaine are short lived. Yet, the negative effects can overpower a person and destroy his life.

Once addicted, the addict's craving for cocaine is all consuming. Money, food, sleep, appearance, responsibilities, morals, job, school, family and friends no longer matter.

The Destructive Power of Cocaine

They call it the Naked City. It isn't a very large neighborhood; just a park surrounded by about a dozen city blocks. The area gained its suggestive nick-name during the 1970's when glamorous Las Vegas show girls called the area home. The beauties were often found in swimsuits, lounging by swimming pools to escape the neon lights and brutal summer heat.

When I *(Todd)* began patrolling the area in the early 1990's much had changed. The area that once flaunted the city's girly glamour had faded away into an often dark and seedy den of despair. Many still refer to it as the Naked City, despite Las Vegas' attempts to alter the area's image by referring to the neighborhood as "Meadows Village."

Most of us working the area were amused by the name change. The narrow, trash-riddled city streets surrounded by concrete patios and desert dirt certainly didn't look like a meadow any of us had ever seen. Run-down apartment buildings and stripped cars littering the streets do not a meadow or a village make.

Despite the deplorable living conditions in the neighborhood, there were many decent and hard-working families that called it home. Kids played and laughed in the park during the days while their parents grilled hot dogs and hamburgers. But as day gave way to night, those families became prisoners in their own homes.

After dark, drug dealers and users lay claim to the neighborhood. The blood from stabbings and gun battles stained the sidewalks as a result of the drug trafficking. Despite the shootings and stabbings, foot chases and fights, I came to know the real people who suffered the devastation of drug use.

I often spent more than forty hours a week in the neighborhood. Working in Meadows Village gave me access to a cast of characters who taught me more about drug use than I could have ever learned in any book or class. More than ten years have passed since I worked the area, but I haven't forgotten some of the people I met while working the Naked City.

One such unforgettable man was John. I felt as if I saw and talked to him more each week than I did with my own wife. By the time I met John, he had racked up felony convictions, spent time in prison and was jobless and homeless. His pedigree told a story of a degenerate drug addict and career criminal. But the more John and I talked, the more I sensed something unique about him. Despite his lengthy and sometimes violent police record, John was polite and respectful when I stopped him to inquire if he had drugs and conduct a records check for outstanding arrest warrants.

We developed a mutual understanding of one another's position in life, and it opened the door to a certain trust and openness. John was what is referred to as a "crack head." His driving motivation in life was to find a way to stay high on crack cocaine. I don't believe anyone ever intentionally becomes hopelessly addicted to any drug, so one day I asked John how it all started for him.

He explained that he was once a successful chef at a large hotel in a small southern town, and his wife was a teacher. But the thought of moving to Las Vegas provided an excitement that maybe there was even more success waiting for them.

John quickly found a well-paying job at a casino. They bought a beautiful home, had nice cars and all the things most people want in life. His wife retired from teaching and enjoyed the freedom of escaping the daily grind. This new-found freedom opened the door to a new circle of friends, and one of them introduced her to crack cocaine. The drug made her feel excited and alive. But John watched in dismay as the drug began to take its toll on their relationship. So he developed a plan. He would try cocaine so he could tell his wife he didn't like it, and they both should quit.

His best intention became his worst nightmare. Cocaine had him in its snare, and he couldn't break free. His drug use affected his work performance and made him unreliable. He soon lost his job, then his home; and then he eventually lost the thing he was trying hardest to hold on to when he first tried the drug – his wife! His despair led him to use more. In order to support his drug habit he began committing crimes.

Crack cocaine provides an immediate and intense rush from just one hit. Many users describe the feeling to be 100 times more intense than an orgasm. However, the effects are very short lived.

I was curious about how often a crack head needed to use the drug, so I asked John how many times a day did he "hit the pipe." I wasn't prepared for his answer; as many as 400 times a day. That is a powerful addiction!

John is haunted by memories of his life before drugs became his reason for living. If only he could have his old life back! But breaking such a powerful addiction requires incredible will power and determination, and John doesn't feel as if he has either. The last time I saw John I was filled with incredible sadness because I had no way of helping him. Cocaine destroyed a good man by changing him into a hopeless addict.

The Addictive Power of Cocaine

Cocaine is so addictive that when animals in test labs are given the option of food and water or cocaine, they always choose cocaine. They will also endure electrical shocks just to get more cocaine. Within days they lose substantial body weight and within a month, they die.

> **Cocaine never leaves a person satisfied.
> It only leaves them wanting more.**

Street Names for Cocaine

There are literally hundreds of names for cocaine. Some of the more common names are: 24-7, Barbs, Bass, Big C, Black Rock, Blow, Candy Cane, Candy Sugar, CDs, Cloud, Coke, Cookies, Dice, Double Bubble, Dust, Electric Kool-Aid, Fat Bags, Foo Foo, Hard Rock, Hotcakes, Icing, Lines, Mojo, Nose Candy, Oyster Stew, Toot, Paradise, Pearl, Rock, Scorpion, Seven-Up, Snow Coke, Tornado, Twinkie, Yam.

The History of Cocaine

Cocaine comes from the Erythroxylon Coca plants found primarily in Colombia, but also in Bolivia, Peru and Ecuador. For thousands of years, Indians from South America experienced a mild high giving them the stamina to work long, hard hours simply by chewing the leaves of the Coca plant. In 1860, pure cocaine was extracted from the leaves; and the medical profession realized it caused a numbing effect. Soon cocaine was being used as an anesthetic and treatment for various illnesses.

Cocaine was also used in various specialty drinks. Coca Wine became popular in the 1800's. In 1886, another invigorating drink called Coca-Cola hit the streets, dubbed as a brain tonic. The original Coke was a refreshing, non-alcoholic drink with a mixture of caffeine and cocaine. The cocaine was removed from the Coca-Cola recipe in 1906.

Until the early 1900's, a person could actually purchase cocaine over the counter in department stores, including Harrods. In 1914, cocaine was declared illegal in the U.S. by the Harrison Narcotic Act.

The use of cocaine exploded in the late 1970's through the '80's. Much of the popularity for the drug was fueled by misinformation. A 1977 article in a widely published and respected news magazine stated cocaine was not addictive, not harmful, did no mental or physical damage, and when used in moderation, it was safer than cigarettes or alcohol. Nearly ten years passed before the same publication wrote articles describing the truth about the drug.

Different Forms of Cocaine

Cocaine has changed significantly since the early days of chewing the leaves for a mild high. Today cocaine is a powerful drug sold illegally around the world in three different forms:

1. Powder – Hydrochloride Salt

Cocaine is taken out of the Coca plant and then manufactured into its final product. The result is an odorless, white, crystalline powder called cocaine hydrochloride. It is 80 to 90 percent pure cocaine along with a few impurities including gasoline, kerosene and benzene. Once the drug leaves South America, it is passed down to various drug exporters, importers and drug dealers. During this journey, various ingredients including sugar, cornstarch, talcum powder and/or amphetamines are added to increase the quantity and the profits. By the time it hits the streets, cocaine is usually less than 50 percent pure. But as mentioned several times before, no user ever really knows what he's taking when he indulges in an illegal drug.

The powder form of cocaine is most often sniffed through the nose, which is referred to as snorting. Water can also be added to the powder to make an intravenous concoction, which increases the risk of HIV, hepatitis and other diseases. Powder cocaine can't be smoked, which is one reason users will convert the powder to freebase cocaine.

2. Freebase Cocaine

Freebase cocaine was developed in the 1970's because of concern over the impurities in the powder form of cocaine. A user makes freebase by mixing highly flammable solvents with the cocaine in a dangerous and time-consuming process. The finished product is a much purer form of cocaine, which is smoked. However, the term "smoked" is misleading because cocaine isn't actually smoked in the same way a person smokes a cigarette or marijuana joint. Freebase cocaine has to be heated and vaporized in a special pipe or burned on a piece of tin foil. The user inhales the fumes from the pipe or foil. This method allows the purest form of cocaine to enter the bloodstream; and it is therefore the most dangerous.

> **In 1980 comedian Richard Pryor set himself on fire while preparing freebase cocaine, resulting in third-degree burns over 50 percent of his body.**

3. Crack Cocaine

Crack cocaine is the newest form of freebase cocaine. It hit the streets in 1985 and has been a serious problem ever since. The major difference in crack cocaine and freebase cocaine is that instead of using all the explosive solvents to remove the impurities, a simple solution of boiling water and either baking soda or ammonia are added to the original cocaine hydrochloride. The solid substance left after the water evaporates resembles small rocks or rock salt. These little crystals are then smoked in a pipe or burned on foil. They make a crackling sound as they heat up – hence the term, crack cocaine. The user inhales the fumes and the vapors reach the brain almost instantaneously. Crack cocaine is 75 to 90 percent pure, making it extremely addictive.

What You Get for Your Money

Crack cocaine is the most addictive form of cocaine on the streets today. Yet it only costs around $10 to $20 per rock. Inhaling crack provides an immediate, intense high that lasts 5 to 10 minutes. The high from snorting is not as intense, but lasts 15 to 20 minutes and can cost anywhere from $20 to $200 per gram.[1]

While the cost for one hit of cocaine may sound relatively cheap, it can quickly become an extremely expensive habit. A person who goes on a binge may consume 40 or 50 rocks a day. The binge might last for several days, which can cost hundreds, perhaps thousands of dollars. Obviously a person who spends so much time using cocaine isn't going to be able to hold down a job. Like many other frequent drug users, cocaine addicts often revert to lying, cheating, stealing and even prostituting to support their habit.

> **Cocaine is God's way of telling you that you make too much money.**
>
> *Robin Williams*

Side Effects of Cocaine

Besides being highly addictive, cocaine can also cause a number of life-threatening problems. These include high blood pressure and constriction of blood vessels resulting in seizures, stroke, heart attack, and respiratory failure. A cocaine overdose can kill an otherwise healthy person. In fact, first-time users can die – making their first experience with cocaine their last.

Cocaine Terms

The following are definitions of common terms used by cocaine users:

- Back to back – smoking crack after injecting heroin
- Bag bride – a crack-smoking prostitute
- Biscuit – 50 rocks of crack cocaine
- Belushi – cocaine and heroin
- Blunt – cocaine and/or marijuana inside a cigar
- Buda – high-grade marijuana joint laced with crack cocaine
- Chasing the dragon – heating up cocaine on a piece of tinfoil
- Chalked up – a person under the influence of cocaine
- Cocoa puff – smoking cocaine and marijuana
- Coke bar – a bar where cocaine is openly used
- Coolie – a cigarette laced with cocaine
- Cracker Jacks – a crack smoker
- Crack house – a location where crack cocaine is sold and used
- Dusty Roads – cocaine and PCP

Flamethrowers – a cigarette laced with cocaine and heroin

Frisco Speedball – cocaine, heroin and LSD

Go on a sleigh ride – inhaling cocaine

Hitch up the reindeers – inhaling cocaine

Line – snorting a single dose of cocaine

Moon rock – crack mixed with heroin

Murder one – cocaine and heroin

Ocean Spray – salt water in a bottle used to spray the nasal passages after snorting cocaine.

Outer-Limits – crack cocaine and LSD

One and One – snorting cocaine with both nostrils

Sandwich – a layer of heroin sandwiched between two layers of cocaine

Shaker-baker-water – materials used to freebase cocaine (shaker bottle, baking soda and water)

Snowball – a combination of cocaine and heroin

Space blasting – smoking cocaine and PCP together

Wicky Stick – PCP, marijuana and crack

Yeyo – Spanish term for cocaine

Breaking the Habit

Getting high on cocaine is easy. But, escaping its addictive power is extremely difficult – impossible for many. The time it takes to kick the addiction varies from person to person, and the treatment is expensive. Some cocaine users may be able to quit with little difficulty, but there is no guarantee that someone won't become addicted for life after trying the drug just one time.

There is no medication to treat cocaine addicts, although researchers are diligently working to find one. Anti-depressants and various medications are often prescribed to help with the depression, mood swings and paranoia that occur during withdrawal.

INVOLVED: Parents' Connection to Drug Prevention

Symptoms
- Drop in grades
- Loss of interest in school, family and friends
- Decreased appetite
- Weight loss
- Dilated pupils
- Talkative
- Blurred vision
- Blood-shot eyes
- Tremors or twitching
- Dizzy
- Headaches
- Coughing or runny nose
- Fever
- Nausea
- Vertigo
- Irritability
- Depression
- Anxiety
- Paranoia
- Insomnia
- Hallucinations
- Increased heart rate
- Increased blood pressure
- Permanent damage to the lungs
- Chest pains
- Shortness of breath
- Seizures
- Stoke
- Heart attack

Cocaine Detection

A urine test can detect cocaine for two to four days in casual users. In chronic users, urinary detection is possible for as long as three weeks.

Cocaine Paraphernalia

Although it's illegal to sell cocaine paraphernalia, it doesn't appear to stop people from buying. The necessary supplies can be purchased over the Internet and through mail-order businesses. They're also frequently sold at tobacco shops, trendy gift and novelty shops and convenience stores. You may have seen a little glass vial with a small flower inside near the register of a convenience store. I often wondered, "Does anyone actually buy those for a wife or a girlfriend?" I don't know the answer to that question; but I have learned that the small glass vials, with the flower removed, of course, are often used as crack pipes.

Common cocaine paraphernalia are:

- Mirrors or glass surface, single-edged razor blades, straws and nasal spray – used for inhaling.
- Syringes, needles, spoons, belts or surgical tubing – used for injection.
- Glass pipes, foil, small glass vials – used for smoking.

Cocaine and the Law

Cocaine is an illegal drug. This means a child or adult could be fined or sent to prison if he is caught in possession of cocaine, using it or selling it.

Cocaine is a Schedule II drug under Federal Law. This means it has high potential for abuse. The legal, pharmaceutical cocaine can be administered by a doctor for legitimate medical uses. It is occasionally used as a local anesthetic for some eye, ear and throat surgeries. Illicit cocaine (clandestinely made) is listed by most states as a Schedule I drug under state laws, meaning there is no lawful use and a high potential for abuse.

INVOLVED: Parents' Connection to Drug Prevention

The Parent Connection

Ideas to Help You Protect Your Child From Drugs

Addiction? Not Me!

Most teens believe they are invincible. When you talk to them about the risks of drugs, they are apt to think: "That would never happen to me." But the truth is people from all walks of life, all races and all ages can become addicts. Many well-known celebrities have not only become addicted to drugs, they have died as a result of their drug use. No doubt they too considered themselves invincible and felt confident this would never happen to them. After all, they had it all – wealth, fame and a bright future. But the truth is, if addiction and death can happen to the rich and famous, it can happen to anyone.

Tip #12 on DRUG PREVENTION is

Help Your Child Understand No One's Invincible.

TRY THIS IDEA!

Who's Who Among the Cocaine Obituaries

Let your child see the reality of the dangers of using cocaine by reading the following "Who's Who Among the Cocaine Obituaries."

John Belushi (age 33) was found dead on March 5, 1982 from an overdose of cocaine and heroin. John was best known for his roles in the "Saturday Night Live" television series, *The Blues Brothers* (with Dan Aykroyd), and *Animal House*.

Leonard K. Bias (age 23) was found dead on June 19, 1986 of a cocaine overdose in his Maryland University dorm room 48 hours after he was drafted by the Boston Celtics in the 1986 NBA Draft. His starting salary was $1 million. Unfortunately, his celebration included cocaine and he never made it to the big leagues.

River Phoenix (age 23) died on the sidewalk of Sunset Boulevard in Hollywood from an overdose of heroin and cocaine on October 31, 1993. He was considered by many to be one of the most promising young actors of his time. River starred in such movies as *Stand By Me, Sneakers;* and he portrayed the teenage Indiana Jones in *Indiana Jones and the Last Crusade.*

Chris Farley (age 33) died from an accidental overdose of cocaine and morphine on December 18, 1997. The day before he died, Chris told friends he had been up four straight days without sleep. Chris was best known for his role in the "Saturday Night Live" television series. He also appeared in *Wayne's World, Coneheads, Billy Madison, Tommy Boy, Black Sheep, Beverly Hills Ninja.* His last movie, *Almost Heroes,* wasn't released until five months after his death. DreamWorks Studio designed the movie and the leading role of "Shrek" specifically for Chris Farley. But because of Chris' untimely death, the voice we now hear as Shrek is Mike Myers.

Robert Lee "Bobby" Hatfield (age 63) was found dead from a cocaine overdose just before a concert on November 5, 2003. Bobby Hatfield and Bill Medley were the duo better known as the Righteous Brothers. Some of their best-known hits were: "You've Lost That Lovin' Feelin," "Unchained Melody" and "Rock and Roll Heaven." The duo was inducted into the Rock and Roll Hall of Fame in March 2003. The initial autopsy listed a heart attack as the cause of death; but after the toxicology report was completed, the cause of death was changed to a heart attack induced by an overdose of cocaine. Sadly, Bill Medley had no idea his singing partner was using cocaine at the time of his death.

Marco Pantani, (age 34) former Tour de France winner, was found dead in a hotel room from a cocaine overdose on February 14, 2004. Death was caused by an increase in blood pressure which resulted in a stroke. In 1998 Pantani, won the Giro d'Italia and the Tour de France – the world's most prestigious cycling tournament.

Kevin DuBrow (age 52) was found dead in his Las Vegas home on November 25, 2007 of a cocaine overdose. Kevin was the lead singer of the heavy metal band "Quiet Riot," which was the first metal band to reach No. 1 on the Billboard chart in the early '80's. In 2004, Kevin recorded a solo album, "In for the Kill." In 2006, his band released, "Rehab."

HERE'S ANOTHER IDEA!
Six Reasons to Avoid Cocaine

Discuss the following reasons to avoid cocaine with your child.

1. A person can become addicted the very first time he tries cocaine.
2. Getting high on cocaine is easy. Escaping its addictive power is extremely difficult – impossible for many.
3. Every positive aspect of cocaine is short lived, and the negative side effects can overpower a person and destroy their life.
4. Once addicted, the craving for cocaine is all-consuming. Money, food, sleep, appearance, responsibilities, morals, job, school, family and friends no longer matter.
5. People addicted to cocaine often spend hundreds, perhaps thousands, of dollars on drugs every day.

6. People wasted on cocaine won't be able to hold a job. There's a good chance they will revert to lying, cheating, stealing and/or prostituting to support their habit.
7. First-time users can die – making their first experience with cocaine their last.

HERE'S AN INTERESTING IDEA!

The following anonymous poem is an amazing description of the power of cocaine and can make a lasting impression on your child. (Warning: some of the words are graphic. Please read it and make sure it is appropriate for your child.)

My Name is Cocaine
(anonymous)

My name is Cocaine - call me Coke for short.
I entered this country without a passport.
Ever since then I've made lots of scum rich.
Some have been murdered and found in a ditch.
I'm more valued than diamonds, more treasured than gold.
Use me just once and you too will be sold.
I'll make a schoolboy forget his books.
I'll make a beauty queen forget her looks.
I'll take a renowned speaker and make a bore.
I'll make a schoolteacher forget how to teach.
I'll make a preacher not want to preach.
I'll take all your rent money and you'll get evicted.
I'll murder your babies or they'll be born addicted.
I'll make you rob and steal and kill.
When you're under my power you have no will.
Remember, my friend, my name is "Big C".
If you try me just one time, you may never be free.
I've destroyed actors, politicians and many a hero.
I've decreased bank accounts from millions to zero.
I make shooting and stabbing a common affair.
Once I take charge you won't have a prayer.
Now that you know me what will you do?
You'll have to decide, it's all up to you.
The day you agree to sit in my saddle.
The decision is one that no one can straddle.
Listen to me, and please listen well.
When you ride with cocaine you are headed for hell!

Reference

[1] Executive Office of the President, Office of National Drug Control Policy, *Cocaine,* November 2003.

Chapter 13

Methamphetamine

> Methamphetamine is a man-made, highly addictive, brain-altering stimulant that accelerates the mind to speeds faster than it was designed to go.

From the lakes of Minnesota,
to the hills of Tennessee,
across the plains of Texas,
from sea to shining sea.
From Detroit down to Houston
and New York to L.A...

... no matter where you live meth is there or on its way.

Hopefully, Lee Greenwood forgives us for using a few of his amazing lyrics from the song "God Bless the USA" to describe the methamphetamine epidemic spreading across our nation. But the same passion and emotion expressed in his song will be necessary to take control of and eradicate this hideous drug.

Perhaps no other drug has gripped the attention of our entire nation like Methamphetamine. Whether you live in a big city or a small town, methamphetamine is already there or will be soon. I (Todd) attended a methamphetamine conference where a Drug Enforcement Agent spoke about illegal methamphetamine laboratories. He stated, "I don't know where you live, but I can bet I have been to your neighborhood."

INVOLVED: Parents' Connection to Drug Prevention

My first year as a narcotics detective was a busy one. We seized more than 370 methamphetamine labs. That's right. My colleagues and I often dismantled more than one lab a day – from shabby trailer parks to posh gated communities.

While meth labs are decreasing in Nevada, they are on the increase in America's Heartland. The five states presently holding claim to the largest number of meth-lab seizures by law enforcement are Missouri, Indiana, Illinois, Tennessee, and Iowa.[1]

I first heard of methamphetamine in 1987 while I was stationed with the Air Force in Hawaii. "Ice" was wreaking havoc in the small islands. At that time, the drug was primarily a problem among the members of Asian street gangs. I still remember news reports of how this drug seemed to overtake those who used it, rendering them mindless, violent zombies. Methamphetamine is sweeping across our nation like a tsunami across the Pacific Ocean.

It might be easy for one to dismiss this so-called drug epidemic as mere hype, but that would be a big mistake. I had the opportunity to return and teach a drug class at the Honolulu Police Department after being away from Hawaii for almost 15 years. I was shocked as I drove throughout the island. I saw billboard after billboard announcing "Community Forum on Methamphetamine."

Ice was no longer the drug of choice among just the Asian gangs in Hawaii. It had taken root and was affecting all who lived there. During my visit, an unprecedented nine local TV stations and five radio stations simultaneously aired an hour long, commercial-free program on the methamphetamine epidemic in Hawaii – during prime time! If you or your community are sitting back waiting to see if and when methamphetamine will be a problem, chances are you're too late. It already is.

The Problem with Methamphetamine

Commonly known as meth, speed or crank, this drug is easy to obtain but next to impossible to quit! Meth is highly addictive, cheap to make and cheap to buy. The recipe is easily accessible on the Internet. However, the chemical used in these recipes are more likely to cause a serious explosion than produce the actual drug.

Methamphetamine

The ingredients, costing less than $100, include common household products purchased at grocery stores and hardware stores. A small amount of cold medicine containing pseudoephedrine plus a combination of products such as acetone, paint thinner, kerosene, sulfuric acid can be used to prepare and manufacture methamphetamine.

The majority of methamphetamine is produced in clandestine laboratories. And make no mistake. These are not laboratories like the ones you used in your high school chemistry class. These are crude, unsophisticated laboratories found on a kitchen countertop, in a garage, a basement, a hotel room, a mini- storage unit or a car.

What's *Cooking*?

Even though the drug may seem easy to "cook-up," the combination of volatile chemicals creates a dangerous environment. Not only are the products used to produce meth highly explosive, but the actual process also produces extremely toxic fumes and by-products. One method of manufacturing meth combines red phosphorus and iodine crystals. Iodine crystals nearly always produce gas fumes, which can cause respiratory problems and even death. However, the mixture of the red phosphorus and iodine creates an invisible and nearly undetectable chemical product called phosphine gas. A single breath of this gas can be enough to cause the lungs to collapse and to result in death. This gas, along with other toxic by-products, permeate the walls, carpet, furniture and ventilation ducts, requiring all the contaminated areas to be removed and disposed of by properly trained law enforcement officers and hazardous waste professionals.

You could have a neighbor cooking up volatile chemicals at this very moment, and you would probably never know unless an explosion occurs. Such was the case of an unsuspecting single mother who asked a friend to watch her young son while she went to the store. The child watched television in the downstairs apartment while the friend decided to do a little *cooking* in the kitchen. It wasn't lunch he was preparing; he was mixing up chemicals to make methamphetamine. Perhaps knowing the mother would return soon caused him to speed up the process by bringing the flammable liquid to a boil. The heavier-than-air evaporating fumes were ignited by the flame causing a powerful explosion in the kitchen. Flames shot down the hallway engulfing the apartment in fire. Luckily, the methamphetamine cook grabbed the little boy in his arms and fled the apartment. My partners and I arrived at the apartment to investigate the meth lab as the fire department left the scene. We spent several hours sifting through the burned debris, collecting and disposing of the hazardous chemicals.

Locating the "Big Fish"

The job of a narcotics detective is not as exciting as movies would have you believe. While there are plenty of moments of adrenaline rush, there are many more hours of tedious surveillance. A successful drug buy from an unsuspecting dealer is more than showing up to buy the drugs and making the arrest. In order to find the **stash house** or the **bigger fish** where large amounts of drugs are hidden, hours and hours of surveillance are required.

Such was the case one hot summer evening in Las Vegas. My partner met with a drug dealer to purchase some methamphetamine. The transaction took just a few minutes, but that was only the beginning of a very long night. For more than an hour my partners and I conducted surveillance on the dealer from one side of town to the other to locate the big fish. We finally located the source of the methamphetamine in a nice, middle-class neighborhood just two blocks from an elementary school. The home was typical of many in Las Vegas – a well kept, two-story house on a manicured cul-de-sac. I sat for several hours in front of the house while the search warrant was prepared. Nothing outside the home gave me or anyone else a clue as to what was hidden inside.

We executed the search warrant in the same way we had executed many before. But we weren't prepared for what we found inside the house. As we entered the 2,500-square-foot residence, we immediately observed the barren rooms, void of furniture or light.

The red stains on the carpet and walls caught our attention as we examined the first floor of the house. At the top of the stairs we saw the source of the stains. The entire top level of the home had been converted into a methamphetamine lab. A Drug Enforcement Administration Chemist was flown in from San Francisco to assist in dismantling the lab. He estimated the lab was capable of producing $80,000 of methamphetamine a week. The lab was so toxic my partners and I had to wear full-body biohazard suits and personal respirators while we dismantled the lab inside the house. The rubber gloves I was wearing filled up like water balloons with sweat from my hands caused by the desert heat, necessitating frequent changes.

It took us more than 30 hours to dismantle the lab and remove the contaminated wall board, bathroom fixtures, flooring and air ducts. The amount of debris from the clean-up was so large a hazardous waste company in Los Angeles sent an 18 wheel, semi-truck and trailer to cart off the toxic waste we pulled out of the house. You can imagine the shock and disbelief of the neighbors as we took over the entire block for more than a day to rid the neighborhood of the meth lab.

Not all methamphetamine labs are seized by law enforcement agents who properly dispose of the toxic chemicals. Many methamphetamine cooks simply pour the chemicals down the drain, bury them in a backyard, toss them along the roadside or into a field or dump them into a sewer or nearby river or stream – contaminating whatever is around them. This waste must be cleaned up, often leaving the owner of the property and tax-payers with the clean-up costs.

> **One pound of meth can produce up to 5 to 6 pounds of hazardous waste.**

The good news is that there are fewer small mom and pop meth labs in the United States, thanks to new laws making it more difficult to purchase over-the-counter cold medicines and the other products used to make meth. Unfortunately, large drug trafficking organizations, primarily from Mexico, have filled the void by creating super-labs in remote areas of California and Mexico.

Street Names for Methamphetamine

Blade, chalk, CR, crank, Cristy, crystal, getgo, glass, ice, hot ice, L.A. glass, L.A. ice, lemon drop, meth, quartz, shabu, shards, speed, stove top, tick tick, Tina, tweek, ventana, and yaba

How Methamphetamine is Used

Meth can be snorted, swallowed, injected or smoked. It comes in three forms:

- **Powder** – crystal-like powder that's white or slightly yellow. Poor quality control during manufacture can also produce a less desirable brownish-orange powder referred to as peanut butter. The powder is snorted, swallowed or injected. Each method produces a different type of high. Injecting the drug causes the most intense reaction. Few people believe they will resort to injecting meth when they start using. But the longer they use, the more likely they are to start using the needle.

- **Crystal** – clear or blue-white chunks which resemble small pieces of rock salt or crushed ice. Crystal meth can be smoked in a light bulb that has the screw thread and interior contents removed or a glass pipe that has a bulb at one end with a very small hole on top. Smoking meth may be called **smoking a puddle.** When meth is smoked it melts into a liquid momentarily and then re-crystallizes as it cools. Meth users call this **growing legs**. This type of methamphetamine tends to produce a longer-lasting and more intense high than the powder.

- **Pills** – small reddish-orange or green pills that are sometimes embossed with the logo "WY." These pills are typically called Yaba. They are manufactured in Asia and smuggled into the U.S.

Who's Using Methamphetamine?

Methamphetamine is an equal-opportunity destroyer. First-time users vary in age from 12 up, but the average age to begin use is usually in the early twenties. But do not be fooled by the average age of first-time users. This is a drug you must take seriously and you must tell your child about. Remember, this drug is a serious threat in communities all across the nation.

Getting High on Methamphetamine

Immediately after smoking or injecting methamphetamine the brain is flooded with a sharp increase of dopamine resulting in a pleasurable, intense rush. This initial rush may only last a few minutes, but the overall high can last for 12 or more hours.

The high from snorting meth or taking it in a pill form also results in a high, but not as intense as the rush from smoking or injecting. Snorting produces a high within three to five minutes while pills produce an effect within 15 to 20 minutes.

Although the user initially feels full of life, powerful and in control, the truth eventually comes out. Increasingly larger doses are required to replicate the original high. This can lead to a severe **addiction** with a long list of side effects that can continue for years after the person has stopped using the drug.

The Addictive Power of Methamphetamine

In the beginning, users may just be looking for a quick boost of energy or an escape from the daily grind, but after the first use, few find it easy to escape the clutches of meth. Over time meth destroys the area of the pleasure sensors in the brain. Without the drug, the user is unable to find pleasure at all. Depression and despair take over, which reinforces the need to get high. Once that occurs, methamphetamine is now an all consuming part of that person's life.

The Bizarre Effects of Meth

As methamphetamine use progresses, it is not uncommon for users to remain high on the drug for days or weeks. Because the drug is a stimulant, it reduces the desire to eat and sleep. Users may go for days or even weeks with very little food and without sleep. I *(Todd)* once had a user tell me he went 21 days without sleep. Of course, after staying awake for weeks at a time, when a user crashes he may also sleep for a week or two.

The term **tweaker** refers to a person who uses meth. However, the term more accurately describes the activities of someone who is constantly high on meth and needs to do something with all that excess energy. When we conduct a search for methamphetamine, we often find large piles of electronic equipment taken apart and tweaked into something else.

Just imagine what happens to the body and mind when it goes long periods without rest. The side effects of the drug, along with long periods of no sleep, cause bizarre personality changes in the user. He can be friendly and relaxed one minute and angry, terrified or paranoid the next. Paranoia consumes many long-time users. Cameras might be placed all around the exterior of the house to watch for the police. I (Todd) even heard of a meth user who killed his dog because he believed the canine was responsible for calling the police and reporting his drug use.

The Destructive, Dark Side of Methamphetamine

There is even a darker side to meth. In law enforcement there is a saying, "You can tell how much meth a person uses by the size of the pornography collection."

Jerry, a drug user with whom I had frequent contact, told me *(Todd)* "getting high is not enough. I need sex too. Just about every street prostitute has a drug addiction they're working to pay for. At first, I would pay them for sex until that got too expensive and cut into my own drug money. I slept with girls I knew and some I didn't. But it's hard to find a woman that will put up with crazy, do-everything sex for 12 to 16 hours a day non-stop. So I turned to pornography. That addiction goes hand-in-hand with meth. I would get high and watch porn movies and masturbate for 24 hours straight. When that wasn't enough, I added a second VCR and TV to watch two movies at once. Then I added two DVD players. I was able to play four porn movies at a time. Over a matter of a few years, I had collected thousands of dollars worth of pornography."

Unfortunately, pornography only fills that craving up to a point. There are those who fulfill their sexual gratification by victimizing others. Some say methamphetamine is to blame for creating the sexually deviant beast, while others argue it only awakens what already lies inside. Whichever one is the case, women and young girls are victimized. Some fall prey to violent sexual assault.

Imagine a young woman arriving at her apartment and putting the key into the lock. Suddenly she is hit from behind, and her shirt is pulled over her head. She is pushed into her own home, tied up on her bed and sexually assaulted for several hours before the drug-crazed user turned rapist leaves. Her emotional scars run deep. It's hard to imagine the pain of being sexually brutalized, much less the fear of never feeling safe again in your own home.

On the streets, I hear about other victims of meth users; girls as young as twelve and thirteen who are given methamphetamine by much older men. Since meth lowers inhibitions, the drug is an easy way to allow the predator to take sexual advantage of the girls. They become victims of their manipulator and the drug. Because they took the drug, many are afraid to tell their parents or the police of the abuse. And so the suspect is left to victimize other young and unsuspecting girls.

Women who willfully choose to use methamphetamine also find themselves in dangerous situations. Some men prey on the women by sexually exploiting them while they are under the influence of the drug. Others may have sex out of fear or through coercion and intimidation.

What to Expect from Meth

At first meth will provide:
    A feeling of euphoria
    Increased energy and alertness
    Decreased appetite
    Weight loss
    A feeling of power

Within time meth will provide:
Anxiety
Irritability
Aggression
Depression
Paranoia
Insomnia
Destroyed teeth
Abscesses or sores
Memory loss
High blood pressure
Elevated heart rate
Fatal kidney and lung disorders
Brain and liver damage
Heart attack, stroke and death
Increased risk of HIV, Hepatitis B & C from I.V. drug use and risky sexual behaviors

Methamphetamine Paraphernalia:
Straws
Razor blades
Mirrors
Syringes
Heated spoons
Surgical tubing pipe

Warning signs of methamphetamine:
Decreased appetite
Weight loss and anorexia
Dilated pupils
Dry mouth
Sweating
Tremors

Methamphetamine

Violent rages
Confusion
Insomnia
Excited speech
Increased energy
Fatigue
Paranoia
Hallucinations
Nausea/Diarrhea
Increased body temperature
Shortness of breath
High blood pressure
Increased heart rate
Chest pain
Convulsions

The Parent Connection

Ideas to Help You Protect Your Child From Drugs

Understanding the Teen Brain

- It's one o'clock in the morning, and a 14-year-old girl climbs out of her bedroom window to meet a 17-year-old boy.
- It's Saturday night, and a 16-year-old boy jumps in a car with a drunk driver to go to the next party.

How many times have you thrown your hands up in frustration and asked your teenager, "What were you thinking?" or wondered to yourself, "Where is your brain?" Well his brain is in the same place as yours, but unlike your brain, his brain is not fully developed.

Until the past few years, it was believed the human brain was fully developed by the time a young person reached puberty. Thanks to the modern marvels of new technology, such as magnetic resonance imaging (MRI), scientists can now observe the growth and development of the brain. Perhaps most surprising are the discoveries pertaining to the Prefrontal Cortex, the section of the brain directly behind the forehead. This portion of the brain is often referred to as the Control Center of the brain because this is where all the functions of the brain come together. An even better name for the Prefrontal Cortex might be the *Wisdom Center* because this portion of the brain tells us if the choices we're about to make are good or bad, right or wrong, healthy or unhealthy. This *Wisdom Center* allows us to plan, set priorities, control impulses and weigh the consequences of our actions. Unfortunately, the prefrontal cortex isn't fully wired until a person reaches the mid-twenties.

Without the ability to rely on the *Wisdom Center*, teenagers are left to make decisions with their Amygdala (pronounced uh-MIG-duh-luh). This portion of the brain is known as the *Emotion Center* of the brain and has nothing to do with making wise choices. That's why an intelligent 14-year-old girl may see nothing wrong with climbing out her bedroom window to meet a 17-year-old boy at one o'clock in the morning. Although she might be an outstanding student in school, she doesn't always use good judgment. At this stage in her life, she's working primarily from her emotions; and her emotions are saying, "This is going to be fun!"

This doesn't mean parents are left twiddling their thumbs while they patiently wait for their child to reach the magical age of 25 to be a responsible, mature human being. It is, however, the very reason why you as a parent need to stay closely connected to your children during the teenage years. Remember, your child is functioning from the *emotion center* of the brain. Her brain is constantly sending the message, "If it feels good – do it!" Letting go and giving an overabundance of freedom at this stage in her life is a train wreck waiting to happen.

Instead of allowing your teen cart-blanche freedom, reasonable curfews and boundaries will help to limit some of those emotional decisions from having long-lasting ramifications. As she begins to demonstrate signs of maturity and responsible behavior, those boundaries and curfews can be *gradually* extended.

Brain Development

Brain development begins in the womb. By age four, the brain has reached its full size. But it's around puberty when the brain begins the final stage of development. During this time, new connections in the brain are strengthened as neurons are busily hardwiring together. Other connections that aren't being used are pruned and discarded. Positive experiences during the teenage years can result in healthy brain development. But the reverse is also true. Negative experiences can lead to unhealthy brain development. These experiences will determine which brain cells get connected and strengthened and which brain cells will be pruned and discarded. This will shape who your child will be forever.

For example, young people who are busy with activities such as sports, music, art, theater, academics, volunteer service, scouts

INVOLVED: Parents' Connection to Drug Prevention

and/or an after-school job are forced to learn how to manage their time, set priorities, accept responsibilities, control impulses and emotions, as well as build healthy relationships. But these skills don't come naturally to adolescents who are used to making choices with the emotion center of their brains. Therefore, for healthy brain development to occur, a young person must spend quality time with nurturing parents as well as caring mentors who provide guidance and direction. Positive mentors might include teachers, coaches, a scout leader, a youth-group leader, grandparents, aunts, uncles and/or a boss at an after-school job.

Healthy activities, along with loving parents and caring mentors, can help hardwire strong connections in a young person's Prefrontal Cortex and place her well on her way to becoming a responsible, thinking adult. Then when she does make an unwise decision based on her emotions, such as climbing out her bedroom window at 1:00 o'clock in the morning, a wise parent will take the opportunity to help her think through why this was not a healthy choice. An appropriate consequence will then need to be determined that will encourage her to think twice before repeating the action again.

But just as positive experiences, nurturing parents and mentors can help hardwire healthy connections in the teenage brain, the opposite is also true. A teen who has little parental involvement and spends long hours each day watching music videos and playing violent video games could be focused on a fantasy world of murder, rape, gangs, stealing, drugs, alcohol and sex. These unhealthy, violent experiences could become associated with the connections that will be hardwired in his brain. As a result, he may find it difficult, even impossible, to set priorities and control his impulses and emotions. Instead of growing into a responsible, mature adult, he may be suspended in a world of irresponsible decisions and prone to being involved in abusive relationships.

So this brings us to the next step in the Parent Connection to Drug Prevention.

> **Tip #13 on DRUG PREVENTION is**
>
> Surround Your Child with Positive Mentors.

Methamphetamine

Even though your relationship with your children is the most important one in his life, spending time with other positive role models is also invaluable. As a relationship between your child and a mentor grows stronger, the positive connections in his brain will also be strengthened.

A mentor might be a close family friend, business associate, neighbor or relative. This person should be several years older than your child and share your family values. A mentor might take your child to McDonald's and enjoy a conversation about sports and cars while consuming a Big Mac and fries. A few weeks later they might shoot some baskets and then find themselves in a discussion about the importance of avoiding drugs, alcohol and sex. These types of relationships and positive messages from both you and other caring adults can help hardwire strong connections in your child's Prefrontal Cortex and place him well on his way to becoming a responsible, successful, thinking adult.

Helpful Suggestions

- Be patient with your teenager, but don't excuse misbehavior.

- Stimulate your child's growth of the Prefrontal Cortex with *wisdom thinking*. For example, challenge your child to solve his own problems instead of always trying to fix them for him. This stimulates wisdom skills. For example, don't give him a list of 10 things to do to fix the problem, along with 10 consequences if he doesn't comply. Instead, ask him to explain how he got himself in this situation and how he plans to resolve it.

- Invite your teenager to be an occasional part of your Saturday evening dinner parties, and encourage him to give his opinion on the different topics discussed.

- Make sure the majority of your conversations with your child are focused on enjoyable topics and not disciple.

TRY THIS IDEA!

Three Things Your Child Needs to Know about
METHAMPHETAMINE

Make sure your child understands these three things about methamphetamine.

1. Meth is made from cold medicine and a combination of dangerous products such as acetone, paint-thinner, kerosene, battery acid and brake cleaner.

2. Once a person starts using meth, increasingly larger doses are required to replicate the original high. This can quickly lead to a severe addiction with a long list of bad side effects that can continue for years after the person has stopped using the drug.

3. Meth tends to destroy the pleasure sensors in the brain. Without the drug, the user is unable to find pleasure at all. Depression and despair begin to take over, which almost always leads to a constant need to get high.

References

[1] El Paso Intelligence Center National Clandestine Laboratory, Cited by The U.S. Department of Justice Drug Enforcement Administration (DEA), *Drugs and Chemicals of Concern,* 2007.

Chapter 14

Anabolic-Androgenic Steroids

> Anabolic-Androgenic steroids are natural or man-made versions of testosterone that serve as a shortcut to increased muscle mass, reduced body fat and enhanced appearance.

*And so it is with a great amount of shame,
I stand before you and tell you, I betrayed your trust.*

Those words were spoken by one-time Track and Field Olympic Gold Medalist, Marion Jones. After years of denial, Jones finally pled guilty to lying to federal investigators regarding her use of anabolic-androgenic steroids.

Once labeled as the fastest woman on earth, Jones now carries the label of convicted felon and cheater. She has been stripped of her five Olympic medals, and her name has been removed from the record books. It's as if she never competed in the events.

The public scorn against steroids and the potential negative health effects are well known. So why then do some athletes risk everything to use them? According to a study conducted by the National Center on Addiction and Substance Abuse, athletes who don't use steroids are left with three options:

1. Compete without using performance-enhancing substances, knowing they may lose to competitors with fewer scruples

2. Abandon their quest because they are unwilling to use performance-enhancing substances to achieve a decisive competitive advantage

3. Use performance-enhancing substances to level the playing field[1]

For a high-school athlete, the opportunity to be the star of the team or the chance to play college sports on a full scholarship may seem worth the risk of using steroids. Watching so-called heroes in professional sports successfully shatter world records by using performance-enhancing drugs can leave these kids thinking, "If it works for them, then why not me?"

But steroid use isn't always about sports. According to one study, most users are looking to improve their muscle mass, strength and physical attractiveness.[2] And as you probably suspect, most steroid users are guys. However, there are those occasional girls who turn to steroids as a means of boosting their athletic performance, losing weight or reducing body fat.

No matter what the reason, anyone using steroids over a period of time can be jeopardizing their health. This is particularly true for young people. The list of side effects is long and can include heart attack, stroke, liver cancer, reduced sex drive, sterility and uncontrolled rage. Steroids are illegal because of the health risks and are banned by most professional and amateur athletic organizations including:

International Olympic Committee (IOC)
National Collegiate Athletic Associate (NCAA)
National Football League (NFL)
Major League Baseball (MLB)
National Basketball Association (NBA)
National Hockey League (NHL)

These medical organizations have also taken a strong stand against steroids use:

American Medical Association
American Academy of Pediatrics
American College of Sports Medicine
Academy of Sports Medicine
American Osteopathic

Anabolic-Androgenic Steroids

Street Names

The more common types of anabolic-androgenic steroids are anadrol, durabolin, oxandrin, winstrol, deca-burabolin, dianabol, and equipoise. But on the street, steroids are typically referred to as:

Roids
Juice
Pump
Arnolds
Stackers
Pumpers
Gym Candy
Weight Trainers

Who Uses Steroids?

People using anabolic-androgenic steroids include athletes, bodybuilders, bodyguards and even law-enforcement officers. But fortunately, most teenagers disapprove of steroids. As a result, steroid use is steadily declining among teens. For some overly motivated athletes, however, this particular drug can be extremely tempting.

How Steroids are Taken

Steroids can be taken in pill form or by injection. Body builders often use four to five different types of steroid at a time. This is called **stacking**. Typically steroids are taken in cycles for six, eight or twelve weeks at a time. Then the person stops for a period of time before starting up again. This is referred to as **cycling**. A cycle typically begins with a low dose. Multiple doses are gradually added until the maximum dose is reached. The dose is then slowly reduced again and discontinued for a period of time. This procedure is called **pyramiding**. When faster results are desired, the user may choose to take massive amounts of steroids known as a **megadose**. And when steroids are taken on an inconsistent basis, this is called **shotgunning**.

Anabolic-Androgenic Steroids and the Law

Anabolic-androgenic steroids are only legal in the United States by prescription. However, they are typically smuggled in from other countries or made in the U.S. in clandestine labs for illicit purposes. Then the drugs make their way to the users through a friend, a drug dealer, fellow athletes at health clubs, personal trainers or purchased over the Internet. Although steroids are easy to obtain, it's a federal offense to possess or sell anabolic-androgenic steroids without a prescription. Therefore, anyone who uses or sells steroids – including teens – is breaking the law and can face a fine and/or a prison sentence. One of the easiest ways to obtain anabolic-androgenic steroids is via the Internet. This also happens to be one of the most common ways of getting busted.

Even the first offense for simple possession of anabolic-androgenic steroids is a federal offense punishable by up to a year in prison and/or a minimum fine of $1,000. However, the cost of possessing steroids doesn't stop with a fine or jail time. There are legal fees, which may reach into the tens of thousands of dollars; and a person convicted of steroid possession may also face the suspension of his driver's license. Anyone holding a professional license such as doctors, nurses, CPAs, cosmetologists, counselors and teachers can have their professional licenses suspended and lose their ability to practice in their specific field. And as in the case of Marion Jones, steroid use also leads to public humiliation, loss of income from endorsements and the loss of all achievements gained during the period of steroid use. The maximum penalty for possessing anabolic-androgenic steroids with the intent to distribute is five years' imprisonment and a $250,000 fine.[3]

Legal Steroids

Legal steroids should not be confused with those that are illegal. Legal steroids are used as anti-inflammatory medication to treat problems including asthma, arthritis, tennis elbow and carpal tunnel syndrome. These forms of steroids require a prescription from the doctor and do *not* build muscle.

Some anabolic-androgenic steroids are also available by a doctor's prescription for legitimate medical uses including hormone replacement in testicular cancer survivors, pituitary problems in teens and muscle re-development for post-surgery or cancer treatments.

Anabolic-Androgenic Steroids can Stunt Growth

There is no question steroids can build muscles, but they can also stop bones from growing. The scrawny 15-year-old who's spent a lifetime being the runt in his class might see steroids as a sure-fire way to build the necessary muscles to catch up with the other guys and impress the girls. Since illegal drugs don't come with warning labels, there's a good chance he wouldn't know the very drug he's taking to bulk up could put a screeching halt to any chances of growing taller. Even small doses of anabolic-androgenic steroids can permanently stop bone growth. So a 15-year-old, 5'6" guy who starts using steroids to improve his appearance and athletic performance may not realize he may have just destroyed any hopes of growing taller, even though his genetic make-up may have programmed him to grow several more inches.

Anabolic-Androgenic Steroids may Increase Rage

Testosterone is the hormone that promotes the masculine traits which transforms boys into men. Testosterone lowers the voice, causes body hair to grow, builds muscles and increases aggression. Strong muscles and a healthy dose of aggression are a necessary combination for most successful athletes.

Anabolic-androgenic steroids, on the other hand, provide an artificial form of testosterone. It mimics the natural hormone by increasing muscle mass and aggression. While the added muscles can be extremely helpful to an athlete, the additional aggression can be dangerous. Some users may only experience mild aggression resulting in moderate mood swings. However, some scientific studies suggest anabolic-androgenic steroids may cause an increase in aggression, leading some users to experience an explosive rage commonly known as roid rage.

> "There may be a greater number of cases of anabolic steroid-induced psychiatric illness in this country than had been assumed... These effects may pose a danger not only to the steroid user, but to the public at large."
>
> H. G. Pope and D. L. Katz, Harvard University

Roid rage may have been a factor which contributed to World Wrestling Entertainment star Chris Benoit strangling his wife and choking his seven-year-old son to death before taking his own life. According to toxicology reports, Benoit had roughly ten times the normal levels of testosterone in his system.

Benoit's apparent heavy steroid use may never be scientifically proven to be the causal factor in the murder-suicide. According to the National Institute on Drug Abuse, "The extent to which steroid abuse contributes to violence and behavioral disorders is unknown."[4] The Benoit tragedy, however, certainly keeps the door open for more questions regarding the link between anabolic-androgenic steroids and violence.

Anabolic-Androgenic Steroids can be Addictive

Discontinuing steroid use is difficult, especially for those who have successfully sculpted their body while using enhancement drugs. There's always the thought, "Maybe a larger dose or using a little longer will make me even stronger."

Then there are those who decide it's time to stop using steroids only to find they face **withdrawal symptoms.** For some, they may experience nothing more than mild irritability and nervousness. Others may spend as much as a year suffering with extreme mood swings accompanied by fatigue, loss of appetite, sleeplessness, depression and decreased sex drive. To counteract these problems, some may find themselves popping pain pills, tranquilizers, sleeping pills and/or stimulants just to cope.

Role Reversal

Peculiar side effects such as male and female role reversal accompany many who use anabolic-androgenic steroids. Ironically, males often experience a feminization effect by acquiring enlarged breasts and shrinking of testicles, while females may experience a masculinization effect of dark facial hair, male-patterned baldness and reduction of breasts. Side effects may include:

Possible Side Effects for Males
- Sterility
- Impotence
- Enlarged breasts
- Enlarged prostate
- Shrinking testicles
- Increased risk of prostate cancer
- Difficulty or pain while urinating
- Male-pattern baldness

Possible Side Effects for Females
- Sterility
- Growth of dark facial and body hair
- Male-pattern baldness
- Deepened voice
- Breast size reduction
- Menstrual problems

Side Effects for Both Males and Females
- Acne
- Yellowing of skin
- Bad breath
- Trembling
- Bloated appearance
- Rapid weight gain
- Nausea, vomiting, diarrhea
- Headaches
- Painful joints and muscle cramps
- Weakened tendons and ligaments
- Insomnia
- High blood pressure

- Liver damage and cancer
- Heart attack and/or stroke
- High cholesterol

Possible Behavioral Side Effects for Males and Females
- Feelings of invincibility
- Hallucinations
- Paranoia
- Anxiety and panic attacks
- Intense mood swings
- Extreme irritability, anger and aggression
- Depression and thoughts of suicide

Additional Health Risks

Steroids are often injected into the muscle tissue. If the needles are shared, the user is at risk of transmitting Hepatitis B & C and HIV.

Over-the-Counter (OTC) Supplements

There are a number of OTC supplements that are legal and popular among young athletes and coaches. The manufacturers claim the supplements build muscles, improve strength and stamina without the destructive side effects of steroids. However, these supplements have not been approved by the Food and Drug Administration (FDA); and there are numerous unanswered questions regarding the effects they can have, especially on teens. Some of these products have also been banned by:

The National Football League (NFL)
National Collegiate Athletic Associate (NCAA)
The International Olympic Committee (IOC).

If your child is interested in using OTC supplements or if your child's coach is recommending them, you should consult your doctor for advice. The fact that a supplement is sold over-the-counter doesn't necessarily make it safe, especially for developing young bodies.

The Parent Connection
Ideas to Help You Protect Your Child from Drugs

Building Strong Character Verses Strong Muscles

Athletes are naturally competitive and strive to be the best. Most amateur and professional athletes find success through hard work and good nutrition, but occasionally some choose a short-cut by using anabolic-androgenic steroids. Not only is this illegal pathway to success dangerous to the mind and body, it also creates an unfair advantage to those who use the drug. In other words, using steroids is cheating.

Accusations about famous athletes using steroids frequently headline the news. Each story provides a teachable moment to help your child build strong character.

This brings us to the next tip on the Parent Connection to Drug Prevention:

Tip #14 on DRUG PREVENTION

Help Your Child Develop Strong Character

HERE'S AN IDEA

Have a Family Discussion on Character

Integrity – Honesty – Dependability – Responsibility

1. As a family, read the following character strengths:

   - A person with **integrity** stands up for what he believes is right even when no one agrees with him.

- An **honest** person tells the truth and does not lie, cheat or steal.

- A **dependable** person always does what he says he is going to do.

- A **responsible** person is accountable for his actions, and when he makes a mistake he accepts the blame without making excuses.

2. As a family, discuss the following questions:

    - Does an honest person lie, cheat or steal occasionally?

    - How many lies can an honest person tell before he is considered a liar?

    - How many times can an honest person cheat before he is considered a cheater?

    - How many items can an honest person steal before he is considered a thief?

HERE'S A FEW MORE IDEAS!
What's the Big Deal about Steroids?

Read the following story to your family and then answer the questions at the end. (Note: This could make for a great dinnertime discussion.)

Barry Bonds, Mark McGwire and Sammy Sosa are just a few of the Major League Baseball players who have been accused of using steroids. It might be easy to look at these strong, virile men and wonder, "What's so wrong with using a drug that makes you a better athlete?"

But anyone who looks at former heavyweight boxer Bob Hazelton doesn't have to ponder that

Anabolic-Androgenic Steroids

question long. In 1969 Hazelton began a successful boxing career. He won seven straight fights and then was defeated by George Forman in 88 seconds. At that time, Forman weighed 230 pounds. Hazelton weighed a mere 180 pounds. That's when Hazelton knew he wasn't big enough to be a champion. So who could blame Hazelton when he decided take "vitamins" that were designed to increase muscle mass? And the vitamins worked. Before long he was weighing in at 235 pounds and winning most of his fights.

A few years later Hazelton learned from a doctor that what he had been taking were not vitamins. They were steroids. In 1980 he developed intense pain in his legs from a circulation problem that ended his career. But that didn't stop his steroid use. He liked what steroids did for him, and he continued to bulk up to 320 pounds. Before long the pain in his calves became so severe it hurt to walk. He developed blood clots, hardening of the arteries and suffered two mild heart attacks. Then he battled gangrene in both legs.

Forty-nine operations later, Bob Hazelton found himself sitting in a wheelchair with both legs amputated above the knees testifying to a House Subcommittee on Crime, Terrorism and Homeland Security regarding the devastating complications he experienced from steroid use. Today Bob Hazelton spends his days speaking to high school students on the dangers of steroids.

You might be saying to yourself, "But that's not going to happen to most people who use steroids." And you're right. While many athletes who use steroids do so with little or no apparent side effects, some end up facing serious problems. Just dealing with the withdrawal symptoms is extremely difficult for some users.

Then there's the problem that's become a major point of contention among many sports fans today. To what degree do steroids play in the record-breaking performance of today's professional athletes? Using steroids to enhance muscles can definitely increase a batter's ability to hit home runs. As the home run statistics go up, so does the batter's salary. And what about the batters who refuse to break the law by using steroids? These athletes may never be able to excel at the level of those using steroids. Thus, the use of steroids has paved the way for an unfair playing field for American's favorite pastime sport.

Meanwhile, fans are left wondering if modern-day heroes such as Barry Bonds, Mark McGwire and Sammy Sosa should be cheered for their astonishing achievements or shunned for cheating. (Note: These men have only been accused of anabolic steroid use, not convicted.)

Question

1. What does steroid use have to do with lying, cheating and stealing?

2. Where does your family stand regarding steroid use?

Why Avoid Steroid Use

Make sure your children are aware of the following information regarding the use of steroids.

4 Reasons to Avoid Steroids

1. Anabolic-androgenic steroids are banned by most professional and amateur athletic organizations

2. It is a federal offense to possess or distribute anabolic-androgenic steroids.

3. Using steroids can stunt a young person's growth. Even small doses can permanently stop bone growth, causing a person to never reach their potential height.

4. Steroid use can cause rage. Some people may experience moderate mood swings when using steroids, while others experience explosive rage commonly known as roid rage.

References

[1] National Center on Addiction and Substance Abuse at Columbia University, *Winning at Any Cost*, Sept. 2000.
[2] Jason Cohen, et al., licensee BioMed Central Ltd, "A League of Their Own: Demographics, Motivations and Patterns of Use of 1,955 Male Adult Non-Medical Anabolic Steroid Users in the U.S. 2007," *Journal of the International Society of Sports Nutrition*, 2007 www.jissn.com/content/4/1/12
[3] Department of Justice, February 2004.
[4] National Institute on Drug Abuse, "Anabolic Steroid Abuse: What are the Health Consequences of Steroid Abuse?" *Research Report Series,* September 2006.

Chapter 15

No Magic Wand

There is no magic wand to solve today's drug problem. And there isn't a silver bullet that will guarantee a child won't try drugs or alcohol. But there are many ways parents can minimize the risk. Unless you are shipwrecked on a deserted island, it is not a matter of *if* your child will be introduced to drugs; it is a matter of *when*. Have you done enough to prepare your child for that moment? Let's quickly recap the ways you can help protect your child from drugs.

Tip #1

Stay Connected with Your Child

The foundation for all successful relationships is commitment. Committing to be *involved* in your child's daily life is perhaps the single greatest thing you can do to prevent your child from using drugs and alcohol. Children who are not connected to and regularly monitored by their parents are four times more likely to use drugs than those children with parents who are connected and who monitor their activities.[1]

Sharing activities such as going to the movies, camping, attending a sporting event or even playing video games are some ways to stay *involved* with your child. Something as simple as regularly eating dinner as a family significantly decreases the likelihood of your children smoking cigarettes, drinking alcohol and using marijuana. And when the chance of your children using those three substances is reduced, the chance they will use other illicit drugs such as cocaine, heroin and methamphetamine is greatly minimized.

INVOLVED: Parents' Connection to Drug Prevention

Tip #2

Dream with Your Child about a Bright Future

While an elementary aged child may have big dreams of becoming Spiderman some day, by junior high, those dreams tend to become a little more realistic. It is important to come alongside your child during this time and encourage their dreams. Not only does this keep you connected to your child, but your encouragement helps keep your child connected to you.

And then there's high school – the time when dreams should be flourishing and diligently pursued. Instead, this is when many teens are focused on risky. Help your child discover his interests and find ways to encourage him to fulfill his goals. A young person who is focused on a bright, exciting future is far less likely to turn to drugs and alcohol. Help your child stay high on life so he won't feel the need to get high on drugs.

Tip #3

Teach Your Child to Care about the Cost of Substance Abuse

Can you ever recall having a conversation with your parents about global warming when you were growing up? If you are like me, the answer is, "Never heard of such a thing back then." Unlike past generations, today's children are growing up in a world where the topics of climate change and going green are everywhere – from the classroom to the big screen.

(Todd) Just recently my 14-year-old son and I were driving in the car listening to a discussion on the radio about global warming. I was shocked at the dialogue *he* initiated about his concerns for the planet and what we should be doing to protect our world.

Regardless of which side of the debate you are on regarding global warming and its causes, one thing is apparent: the topic is generating a great desire among young people to take better care of our world than past generations have. And that's a good thing.

So what do global warming and drug use have in common? Well, nothing, except we should be doing as much to educate our children about the impact of substance abuse on our communities as we are teaching them about the impact of global warming on our environment.

The emotional and financial impact of substance abuse is staggering. Every year millions of Americans lives are changed by the destructive power of drugs and alcohol. And the annual economic cost of drug and alcohol abuse reaches into the hundreds of billions of dollars. Teaching your child to care about the cost of substance abuse is a first step in causing younger generations to tackle the substance-abuse problem in our country head on.

- Do you and your child want to do something to prevent child abuse and neglect? Then get *involved* in preventing the abuse of alcohol and drugs!

- Do you and your child want to do something to reduce crime in your community? Then get *involved* in preventing the abuse of alcohol and drugs!

- Do you and your child want to help save lives of thousands of Americans every year? Then get *involved* in preventing the abuse of alcohol and drugs.

Teaching your child to care deeply about these issues will empower her to become part of the solution and not part of the problem.

Tip #4

Talk About Drugs Early and Never Stop

Wouldn't you like to know the exact date, time and place your child will first be introduced to drugs and alcohol? If you knew that information right now, when would you start to prepare your child? A day in advance? How about a week? Maybe a year?

In other words, how much time will be required to provide your child with the ability to confidently say the words, "No thanks. I don't do drugs."

This isn't going to occur in days or weeks. This type of training will take years. And don't forget…

INVOLVED: Parents' Connection to Drug Prevention

By the 8th grade:[2]

39 percent have consumed alcohol
22 percent have smoked cigarettes
16 percent have used inhalants
14 percent have used marijuana

Preparing your children far in advance of that first offer is imperative. With each passing year, kids face difficult situations which put them at greater risk of trying drugs. The transitions between elementary and middle school and again into high school cause new academic and social challenges. Throw in a move to a new school, problems in relationships or parents in the midst of a divorce, and the risk of drug use continues to escalate.

Middle school is where most teens are first exposed to cigarettes and alcohol. During the high school years, the availability of drugs, along with peer pressure to experiment with drugs increases.[3]

As previously discussed, the teen brain is still in a developmental stage. Teens' judgment and decision-making skills limit their ability to make reasonable risk assessments and sound decisions. That's why it's crucial you stay *involved* in your child's life and support him as he learns to maneuver into the adult years.

Remember, when young people learn about the risk of drugs from their parents, they are 50 percent less likely to try drugs than children who didn't get drug information from their parents.[4]

Tip #5 – #7

Teach Your Child Your Values Regarding #5 Drugs, #6 Tobacco and #7 Alcohol

Values are those concepts that are near and dear to your heart. For many people, their values draw the line between right and wrong. There is no in between. Telling the truth, being honest, never stealing are values many parents strive to instill in their children. Values are not learned over night. But when children are consistently taught by words and actions, this provides the very foundation for the person your child will become.

Values regarding drugs are no different. Where you stand on this subject and the passion you demonstrate while sharing your values will also shape the foundation of your child's life. Training must start early and include both words and actions. Remember, actions speak far louder than words – and your child is watching!

Peer pressure, outside influences and today's culture play a significant role in a child's everyday life. If you don't clearly define your values on substance abuse then you allow your child's values to be shaped by the media, Hollywood celebrities, acquaintances and friends. More than two-thirds of teens ages 13 to 17, however, say upsetting their parents or losing the respect of family and friends is one of the main reasons they don't use drugs.[5] Your values do make a difference!

Tip #8

Find Teachable Moments

Talking to your child about the dangers of drugs and explaining your values on substance abuse are critical components in keeping your child drug free. It is one thing to sit down and tell them, "Don't do that because this could happen." It is another thing to sit down and talk to them about an incident that recently happened in your community, in their school or in your family. Be sure and take advantage of all teachable moments.

For younger children, teachable moments might come as you paint your child's bedroom or have him read warning labels out loud. Teachable moments for older children might arise while attending a rock concert together and striking up a conversation about the unmistakable aroma of marijuana in the air. Another teachable moment might come after Uncle Joe gets drunk at the family picnic.

Teachable moments are often as close as the local or national news. Take a look at these headlines and think about the media circus they create: "Paris Arrested for DUI." "Britney Loses Kids Over Drug Use." "Anna Nicole Dies of Drug Overdose." "Heath Ledger Dies from Accidental Overdose." Unfortunately, the media coverage of such events is focused on celebrity gossip rather than the cause of the actual tragedy – substance abuse. Transform news-breaking events into teachable moments to reinforce your values on substance abuse.

Tip #9

Be Prepared to Answer the Question, "Did you use Drugs?"

Nearly half (45.5 percent) of Americans have tried illicit drugs at least once in their lifetime.[6] So the chances are about 50/50 that you have tried an illegal drug at least once in your lifetime.

For half of you reading this book the answer to, "Did you ever use drugs?" is a simple, "No, I didn't."

But don't stop there. Explain why you chose not to use drugs. Was it a lifelong dream you were pursuing that caused you to say no? Was it the fear of disappointing your parents? Discuss the reasons for why you chose not to use drugs along with the benefits of your choice. Also talk about the difficult situations you may have encountered because of that choice. Sometimes doing the right thing isn't always the easy thing. Losing friends or invitations to be with the cool crowd sometimes follows the decision to *just say no*. Help your children understand the rewards of not disappointing parents, getting arrested or becoming addicted are definitely worth their brave decision.

If you did use drugs, don't let this prevent you from taking a strong stand against drugs. Your silence can be detrimental to your child's future! Today's youth have access to a drug culture and drug misinformation like never before. You can't allow your past to prevent you from being *involved* in your child's present life and future.

Remember, it's important not to glorify your past drug experiences by taking a trip down memory lane. But your willingness to share your regrets and the negative consequences you encountered could reinforce your values.

> Our children don't expect us to be perfect.
> But they appreciate parents who can talk
> honestly about difficult situations.

Tip #10

Regularly Monitor Your Child's Computer

"Don't talk to strangers" was my mother's standing order. It was pretty simple to follow that rule. My entire world consisted of friends in my neighborhood. However, today's kids are running around in virtual neighborhoods on Internet websites such as MySpace and Facebook. Talking to strangers is just part of what is now called *social networking*.

There are more than 212 million Internet users in the United States (70 percent of the population) according to Neilson Online and more than one billion web pages. Of course, the Internet has many legitimate uses. However, it also provides your child instant access to drugs, pornography and sexual predators looking to entice their next victim. If you don't monitor who your child is talking to on the Internet and the websites they are viewing, the time to start is now.

I (Todd) worked a case on an Internet drug dealer with the NYPD several years ago. An NYPD narcotics detective set up an undercover account online and began purchasing drugs from someone who represented himself as a pharmaceutical distributor. The distributor was actually an unemployed restaurant worker who created a bogus company and website to sell drugs. The detective was able to purchase several types of controlled substances and illegal drugs from more than 2000 miles away with just a click of the mouse.

The NYPD detective and I verified the drug dealer lived in Las Vegas. Together we served a search warrant on the drug dealer's house. Inside we found extensive records of his online drug sales activities along with several types of illegal drugs. He had complete ledgers with the names, addresses and photo identification of all of his clients in more than twenty states. The suspect sold drugs to hundreds of high school students and kept copies of the kids' drug requests on official looking letterhead. As hard as it is to believe, he even kept copies of the identification they sent, many of which were copies of their student ID's.

Fortunately that drug dealer ended up in prison in New York for nearly three years. After his release in New York, he spent four more years in a Nevada prison. However, the Internet is still overrun with people just like this who sell drugs to anyone with money.

Access to a credit card is all your child needs to purchase prescription drugs from online pharmacies.

Regularly monitoring your child's computer is smart parenting.

Tip # 11

Wait Up for Your Child

Imagine your 15-year-old son creeping quietly into the house on a Saturday night trying desperately not to awaken you. As his head hits the pillow, he's still flying high from the effects of his first encounter with marijuana. He's already looking forward to next weekend when he can do this again. Of course, he has no concerns about you catching on to what he's up to … because you're always asleep when he gets home.

Imagine waking up the morning after your daughter's first date with her new boyfriend and learning that when she refused his sexual advances he tore her clothes and physically abused her. When she came home you weren't available to hold her, comfort her and call the police … because you were asleep.

Imagine waking up in the morning and finding your teenage son never came home the night before. Frantically you call his friends and learn he left the party before midnight. Then you get the phone call from the police informing you your son's car evidently veered off a dark, winding road and hit a tree sometime before midnight. Your son was unconscious in the car when a truck driver spotted the wreckage around daybreak and called the police. Had you only waited up, you would have known he was in trouble.

Waiting up for your children is a form of sacrificial love. Knowing you will be up when they come home may be the very reason your children say no to drugs and sex.

Tip #12

Help Your Child Understand No One's Invincible

Can you look back in time and think of some really dangerous or stupid things you did? A few years ago I (Todd) was sitting on surveillance near a set of train tracks. A train pulled into the area and stopped near where I was parked. As I looked at the engine and cars of the train, it took me back to when I was a child and lived near train tracks. When I was seven years old, my brother, who was thirteen, would hop the trains and ride them downtown. Of course, desiring to be like my older brother, I wanted to ride the trains too. I wasn't fast enough or tall enough to run along the train and jump on by myself, so my brother would jump onto the train first. I would wait down the tracks and start running as he approached. When he was close enough, I would jump up to the ladder on the side of the train car; and my brother would grab hold of me to make sure I didn't fall off.

I don't ever remember thinking that what I was doing was dangerous or that I could die if I fell under the train. That is, until I was sitting on that surveillance and I began thinking about what if one of my sons was trying to hop the train.

Whether the reason is lack of maturity, limited life experience or just plain ignorance, many kids believe they are invincible. They think, "Bad things only happen to other people." And "it will never happen to me."

I have never arrested one person who told me, "I knew when I did this you would catch me." I have never met one drug addict (and I have met a lot of them) who said to me, "I always knew I was going to lose everything and be a junkie someday." All of them thought, "I'm in control. I can quit anytime." It's that false sense of control that leads many down the path of destruction.

Look for opportunities in the news and in your own life experiences to discuss events and tragedies with your child that help them understand bad things do happen to good people.

Tip #13

Surround Your Child with Positive Mentors

Parents play a critical role in mentoring their children; but how fortunate for both the parent and child when other adults with strong character enter that child's life as a positive role model.

(*Todd*) I didn't have a dad around when I was growing up, so it was my godfather Jim who had the most influence in shaping my desire to be a police officer. Jim was the chief of police in the town where I grew up. Sometimes after church he would take me for a drive around town in his unmarked police car. Everywhere we went people smiled and waved at Jim. They didn't just like him because he was the chief of police, they liked him because he respected and cared about the people he served. I only had the opportunity to spend a few hours a month with Jim when I was growing up, but even that short amount of time had a profound impact on my life. I remember thinking from a very young age, "When I grow up, I want be just like Chief."

It was that desire and his influence that helped me say no to drugs that day at the bus stop when the guy handed me a marijuana cigarette and said, "You want to try it, kid?"

Jim retired several years ago. I recently had the opportunity to take him to work with me and drive him around the city in my police car. It was one of the proudest days of my life. That man had a profound impact on my life. Without his friendship, I wouldn't be the man I am today.

Never underestimate the powerful impact a positive mentor can have in shaping your child's choices and future.

Tip #14

Help Your Child Develop Strong Character

People often talk about having character, but have you really sat down with your child and talked about what that means?

Merriam-Webster's Dictionary Online defines character as, "One of the attributes or features that make up and distinguish an individual." In his booklet, *Making Ethical Decisions,* Michael Josephson, founder of *Character Counts* writes; "Character is not the same thing as reputation. Character is what you are. Reputation is what people say you are. Abraham Lincoln likened character to a tree and reputation to its shadow."

Expanding on that concept, consider the following illustration. Two neighbors planted new trees in their yards. The first neighbor placed his tree in a shallow hole, gave the trunk no support, yet he watered and fertilized it infrequently. Strong winds often caused the trunk to bend and sway. Its roots were thin and unable to provide a strong anchor for the tree. The tree's growth was slow, and its trunk grew crooked. Its branches were thin, its leaves were sparse and sunlight passed right through.

The second neighbor planted his tree into a deep hole which allowed the roots to grow deep into the soil. The trunk was supported by two stakes which provided constant support and prevented it from being knocked down by the winds. This tree was also watered and fertilized regularly. The tree grew quickly, and its roots provided a solid foundation. The trunk grew thick and straight, and it supported an expansive canopy of branches and leaves. The tree's lush canopy cast cooling shade on the ground below.

A child's character is formed and grows largely according to the values and support his parents provide. It's the parent's responsibility to instill the values that can develop strong character traits such as integrity, honesty, dependability and responsibility. As you nourish your values with solid actions and beliefs, your children will have a far greater chance of successfully establishing strong roots for a solid foundation. This will in turn empower your children to stand firm in the midst of difficult situations. And as they grow and mature from their good choices, as well as their mistakes, their character can strengthen and become a source of encouragement and inspiration for all those who share their life.

Stay
Involved.

INVOLVED: Parents' Connection to Drug Prevention

References

[1] Metzler, Rusby, & Biglan, *"Community Builders for Success: Monitoring After School Activities,"* Oregon Research Institute, 1999.
[2] Ibid.
[3] National Institute on Drug Abuse, "Science of Addiction," NIH Pub No. 07-5605, April 2007.
[4] Partnership for a Drug-Free America, *Partnership Attitude Tracking Study*, 2003.
[5] Partnership for a Drug-Free America, *Partnership Attitude Tracking Study*, 2005.
[6] Substance Abuse and Mental Health Services Administration, *Results from the 2006 National Survey on Drug Use and Health: National Findings*, 2007.

Other Drugs of Abuse

The previous chapters discussed the most commonly abused drugs in detail. Although an entire chapter is not devoted to the following drugs, it is important they not be overlooked. In some cases, hundreds of thousands of children use them annually.

Amphetamines are stimulants that speed up the central nervous system similar to the natural hormone found in humans called adrenaline. There are three types of amphetamines: methamphetamine, dexamphetamine and amphetamine. People using amphetamines feel alert, awake and talkative. Amphetamines come in powder, pill or capsules and can be swallowed, snorted, injected or sniffed. Amphetamines can cause increased blood pressure as well as increased breathing and heart rate. Abusing amphetamines can result in irritability, insomnia, depression, paranoia, impulsive behavior and aggression. People abusing amphetamines can easily find themselves dealing with addiction, tolerance and withdrawal symptoms. Other drugs with similar effects are cocaine, ecstasy and caffeine. Common street names include: *speed, uppers, pep pills and crank.* There are also FDA approved forms of prescription amphetamines used to treat Attention Deficit Hyperactivity Disorder (ADHA) and narcolepsy (severe daytime drowsiness) and chronic fatigue syndrome.

Cheese Heroin is cheap, highly addictive and deadly. According to the *Dallas Morning News,* as many as 17 teenagers from Dallas County died after using the drug between 2005 and 2007. Cheese heroin consists of Mexican black tar heroin and cold medicine such as Tylenol PM. The drug is tan in color and packaged in folded pieces of paper or small plastic bags. A single dose, called a bump, goes for about $2 and is snorted through a straw. Although children are the primary targets for cheese heroin, there is nothing childish about the addiction and withdrawal symptoms that occur after using this drug.

Hashish/Hashish Oil, more commonly called *hash,* comes from the resin of the cannabis plant. The THC-rich resinous portions of the plant are dried and pressed together into cubes, balls and cake-like forms. Marijuana also comes from the cannabis plants, but consists of the dried flowers, stems and leaves. Hashish was once considered to be far more potent than marijuana, but that is not always the case today. Hashish, like marijuana can be eaten or smoked.

Heroin is an opiate (narcotic). It's a chemically enhanced version of morphine. Street names for heroin include *dope, smack, Big H, and junk.* It's injected, snorted or inhaled. All forms of opiates have high potential for abuse and addiction. The purest form of heroin is a fine bitter-tasting powder. Heroin varies in color and consistency depending on the origin of the drug. In the southwestern United States, heroin is commonly a brown powder or a sticky black tar-like substance. In the eastern United States, heroin is most commonly a fine white powder. Regardless of the appearance or origin, heroin quickly traps most users into a lifelong battle of addiction and agonizing withdrawal symptoms that include painful cramps and uncontrolled vomiting. Heroin reduces brain activity resulting in depressed, shallow breathing. Even longtime users suffer from accidental overdoses that can result in death. In recent years, heroin has become more popular among teens in some areas of the country.

Ketamine is an FDA approved anesthetic for humans and animals. But when abused, Ketamine has similar effects as PCP. On the streets, Ketamine is known as *Special K, Vitamin K and K.* The liquid forms of Ketamine are injected or poured into drinks. The powder forms can be snorted or added to a marijuana joint or cigarette and smoked. Those abusing Ketamine can experience anything from a mild dreamy numb state to a bad out-of-body hallucinogenic experience known as the *K-hole.* Ketamine is odorless and tasteless and has been reportedly used as a date-rape drug. Ketamine can impair a person's judgment and coordination for up to 24 hours. Users also experience depression and high

Other Drugs of Abuse

blood pressure. An overdose can cause severe brain damage and respiratory problems resulting in death.

LSD is short for Lysergic Acid Diethylamide and is most commonly known on the street simply as *acid*. In the '60's and '70's LSD was known as the psychedelic drug of choice. Although it's lost some of its popularity through the years because of its reputation of bad trips, LSD still remains one of the most common hallucinogenic drugs of today. LSD is colorless and odorless but has a slight bitter taste. It comes in liquid, pill or gelatin form. But the most common way LSD is sold on the street is on small, uniquely designed pieces of perforated blotter paper called tabs. The tabs are soaked in LSD, dried and then placed under the tongue. An acid trip can last around 12 hours and cause the user to experience rich visual hallucinations where he sees, feels and hears things that don't exist. These distorted sensations can cause the user to become frightened and lead to a severe panic attack. A bad trip can cause a user to become extremely violent and do bazaar things such as jumping out a plate glass window or severely hurting himself or others around him. Some users experience recurring flashbacks for more than a year after tripping on LSD. Larger does of LSD can cause convulsions, a coma, heart or lung failure. Although LSD is not considered addictive, users have a tendency to build a tolerance to the drug requiring larger doses to obtain the desired high. Increased doses of LSD are extremely dangerous.

Mescaline is a hallucinogenic drug that comes from the Peyote and San Pedro cactus. Street names include: *button, mesc, devil's weed and cactus*. Portions of the small cactus plant are removed and dried. The remains are then chewed or soaked in water and poured in other drinks to help disguise the disgusting taste. Tripping on Mescaline is typically a milder version of an LSD trip complete with bazaar visual hallucinations, bad trips and recurring flashbacks. Just as with LSD, Mescaline can cause convulsions, heart failure and death. Although Mescaline is not addictive, users often increase the dose because of tolerance.

Methylphenidate is a legal, prescription stimulant used primarily to treat children with Attention Deficit Hyperactivity Disorder (ADHD). Ritalin®, Attenta® and Concerta® are a few of the brand name prescription drugs that contain Methylphenidate. When taken as directed by the doctor, these drugs can enhance brain activity, increased alertness and are not addictive. However, Methylphenidate is in the same family as the illegal street drug, methamphetamine, also known as crystal meth. When Methylphenidate is abused, this wonder drug that helps so many people can quickly become a dangerous addictive drug with serious, even deadly side effects. When users abuse Methylphenidate, they significantly increase the dose and swallow the pills or crush them to make a powder. The powder is then snorted or dissolved in water and injected.

Morphine is an opioid (narcotic). Street names include *morf and dreamer.* It's the most effective pain killer available today, but should always be monitored closely by a doctor. Morphine is injected into the skin, muscle or vein, smoked, sniffed or swallowed. Serious side effects, including death, can occur when Morphine is mixed with other drugs or alcohol. Although it can produce a euphoric high, Morphine can quickly lead to addiction, tolerance and severe withdrawal symptoms.

Mushrooms are actual mushrooms that contain their own hallucinogenic compounds known as psilocybin and psilocyn. They have the appearance of fresh or dried mushrooms and are eaten or brewed as tea. Because of the bitter taste, mushrooms are often eaten with other foods or dipped in something like chocolate or peanut butter. Trips on these magical mushrooms can vary greatly from enjoyable to terrifying. Physical effects can include severe abdominal cramps, nausea, vomiting and diarrhea. With larger doses, the experience is often similar to LSD including visual hallucinations. A bad trip can include recurring flashbacks weeks or months after the experience occurred. Common street names are *shrooms, magic mushrooms and caps.*

Other Drugs of Abuse

Opium is an opioid (narcotic). It comes from the opium poppy plant (primarily from Afghanistan) and is sold on the streets as a powder and solid. It's smoked, eaten or injected. Users experience a euphoric high and drowsiness that can slow breathing and result in unconsciousness. Larger doses may cause a coma or death. Opium is highly addictive and can lead to tolerance and withdrawal symptoms.

PCP is short for phencyclidine. On the street it's referred to as *angle dust*, but don't be fooled by the name. PCP is considered to be among the most dangerous of all illegal drugs. It is available in tablets, capsules, liquid or powder and is snorted, swallowed or smoked. Users often lace a joint of marijuana with PCP powder or create a **wet stick** by dipping their cigarette or joint into liquid PCP. Depending on the amount taken and how it's used, PCP can act as a pain killer, stimulant, depressant or a hallucinogen. The effects of PCP can vary from a euphoric numb sensation to a detachment from one's body. High doses of PCP can result in a seizure, coma and death. Users are prone to extreme violence and suffer with severe depression, delusions, schizophrenic behavior and suicidal compulsive behavior.

Rohypnol is commonly known as *roofies, roach* and *the date rape drug* on the street. It's a sedative that is legal in many countries, but not in America or Canada. It comes in white pills with the label **Roche** and a circled number one or two inscribed on the pill indicating if it's one or two milligram dose. The pills are either swallowed or crushed and added to a drink. Although Rohypnol is in the same pharmaceutical family as Valium, it's about 10 times stronger. A person who is using Rohypnol is said to be **Roached Out**. Sexual predators have been known to slip Rohypnol into an unsuspecting victims drink resulting in a loss of inhibitions and a lapse of memory for several hours. When sedatives such as Rohypnol are combined with alcohol or other drugs such as amphetamines, serious complication can occur including dramatically slowed breathing and heart rate, coma, seizures and death. Using Rohypnol for even a short period of time can lead to problems with addiction, tolerance and withdrawal symptoms.

Types of Drugs

Hallucinogens

Ecstasy
Hashish
LSD
Marinol
Marijuana

Mescaline
Mushrooms
PCP
Peyote

Narcotics/Opioids

Codeine
Heroin
Hydrocodone (Vicodin)
Meperidine (Demeral)

Morphine
Opium
Oxycodone (OxyCotin)
Propoxyphene (Darvon)

Stimulants

Amphetamine
Cocaine
Crack Cocaine

Methamphetamine
Methylphenidate (Ritalin)
Tobacco

Depressants

Alcohol
GHB

Ketamine
Rohypnol

Club Drugs / Designer Drugs

Ecstasy
GHB

Ketamine
Rohypnol